The Importance of Inner Healing and Deliverance for Effective Discipleship

The Importance of Inner Healing and Deliverance for Effective Discipleship

A Working Model for the Local Church

Johnathan Lee Shoo Chiang

Foreword by Dominic Yeo

WIPF & STOCK · Eugene, Oregon

THE IMPORTANCE OF INNER HEALING AND DELIVERANCE FOR EFFECTIVE DISCIPLESHIP
A Working Model for the Local Church

Copyright © 2019 Trinity Christian Centre. All rights reserved. Except for brief quotations in critical publications or reviews, no part of this book may be reproduced in any manner without prior written permission from the publisher. Write: Permissions, Wipf and Stock Publishers, 199 W. 8th Ave., Suite 3, Eugene, OR 97401.

Wipf & Stock
An Imprint of Wipf and Stock Publishers
199 W. 8th Ave., Suite 3
Eugene, OR 97401

www.wipfandstock.com

PAPERBACK ISBN: 978-1-5326-8977-2
HARDCOVER ISBN: 978-1-5326-8978-9
EBOOK ISBN: 978-1-5326-8979-6

Manufactured in the U.S.A. NOVEMBER 15, 2019

Scripture quotations taken from the New American Standard Bible® (NASB), Copyright © 1960, 1962, 1963, 1968, 1971, 1972, 1973, 1975, 1977, 1995 by The Lockman Foundation. Used by permission. www.Lockman.org

Scripture quotations taken from The Holy Bible, New International Version® NIV® Copyright © 1973 1978 1984 2011 by Biblica, Inc. TM. Used by permission. All rights reserved worldwide.

The opinion and views expressed in this book are the author's own and do not necessarily constitute the official stand of the churches involved in his research.

Dedicated to my excellent wife, Margaret Yap Yue Jing. Thank you for being my partner and friend in this ministry journey. You are God's gift to me (Proverbs 19:14; 31:10–31)—love you always.

Contents

List of Diagrams and Tables | ix

Foreword by Dominic Yeo | xi

Acknowledgments | xiii

List of Abbreviations | xvii

Introduction | xix

1 The Need for Inner Healing and Deliverance (IHD) and the Definition of IHD | 1

2 Field Research: A Grounded Theory on IHD and Discipleship Effectiveness | 16

3 Linking Sanctification, IHD, and Discipleship | 45

4 Where Might God be Placing the IHD Ministry? | 71

5 Discipleship that Includes IHD for the Post-Modern Era | 114

6 Conclusion: An IHD Ministry that is Fully Integrated in a Church Discipleship Structure | 130

Appendix A: Sample of Coding Exercise | 137

Appendix B: Sample of Memo Constructed from Coding in Appendix A | 144

Appendix C: Sample Group Category A (Group 1 and 2), Questions on Written Interview to Leaders and Pastors | 148

Appendix D: Sample Group Category B (Group 3)—Written Interview Questionaire | 151

Appendix E: Sample Identifying Benefits from Testimony and Accounts of Each Benefit | 153

Appendix F: Sample Second Count of Benefits According to Types | 157

Appendix G: Longtitudinal Tracking of DEW Participants from a Taiwanese Church | 159

Bibliography | 161

List of Diagrams and Tables

Diagram 1   Behavioral formation | 12

Diagram 2   Formation of sinful unhealthy behavior | 13

Diagram 3   Inner healing: Replacing ungodly beliefs and painful emotions | 13

Diagram 4   Formation of sinful unhealthy behavior involving demonic spirits | 14

Diagram 5   Inner healing and deliverance (removing demonic footholds) | 14

Table 1   10 Elements for Spiritual Formation (Summary of TRACT's 10 elements for spiritual formation) | 122

Foreword

PHYSICAL HEALING IS GENERALLY straightforward. If someone gets a cold, a few days of rest will bring them back into the pink of health. If someone breaks a bone, the area is put into a cast until the bone heals. God made the physical body in such a way that when something is wrong, internal processes kick in to fight off infection and regenerate cells.

But when it comes to spiritual and emotional healing, things get complicated. When someone experiences hurt or trauma, the body doesn't automatically repair painful emotions or bad memories. Instead, it finds ways to get by—coping mechanisms to rationalize the pain or altogether sweep the event under the carpet of their mind. Left unresolved, these hurts rear their ugly head in the form of fears, bad habits, and unhealthy behaviors.

Staying in this place of brokenness is not God's intention for humanity. That's why God works to restore *shalom*—wholeness in body, mind, and spirit. We see this exemplified in the healing ministry of Jesus who came to proclaim freedom to the prisoners, to restore sight to the blind, and to set the oppressed free (Luke 4:18).

There is a constant battle for our mind and heart. However, few are equipped to fight back and overcome. As a result, many Christians continue to get by with life while locked up in the prison of unresolved hurt, unhealthy emotions, and ungodly beliefs. Only when emotional and spiritual healing takes place does one experience true freedom in Christ.

Inner healing and deliverance are not new. Rev Dr Lee spends a portion of the book exploring its prevalence from biblical times to today. However, many methodologies fall short of educating and empowering believers for what takes place during the ministry, as well as life afterward. As a result, this ministry can turn churches into hospitals. Instead of making disciples, they are caring for patients. Instead of multiplying harvest-workers, they continue tending to people who don't seem to get better.

Foreword

While healing and deliverance are important aspects of the church, it must be in service to a church's mandate of making disciples. To be effective, inner healing and deliverance must take a comprehensive and integrative approach. It must go beyond improving a person's current mental, emotional, and spiritual state by evolving into a means of helping understand how they should continue growing in the Lord. That is the core message of this doctoral dissertation-turned-book—a powerful ministry that restores the broken and sets people free to fulfill their God-given destiny.

I have witnessed how Rev Dr Lee has helped many experience tremendous life change. As counselees give their hurt and trauma to the Lord, a divine exchange takes place that enables them to forge forward into lives of freedom, abundance, and purpose. They understand the root cause of their struggles. They personally experience the power and love of God. They are also given the keys to victorious living as they learn how to rebuild their spiritual foundations, develop handles for continued sanctification, and encouraged to pursue ongoing discipleship.

While the ministry was centered on a partnership with the Holy Spirit, I was curious to know how others could be trained for the ministry. Rev Dr Lee was determined to develop a framework that utilized his extensive knowledge and experience—a form of discipleship that integrated formal teaching, prayer, one-on-one counseling, and after-ministry accountability and spiritual growth. As part of Rev Dr Lee's research, ministers from two nations were interviewed to understand how they have benefitted from this framework. Their responses, which can be found throughout this book, attest to a framework and methodology that can be replicated across cultures and contexts.

A man who walks the talk, Rev Dr Lee regularly takes on inner healing and deliverance cases, helping many move out of darkness to live fully and freely in God. He teaches the next generation of disciple-makers as an adjunct lecturer of a multi-disciplinary college where he teaches pastoral counseling. This combination of a pastoral heart and academic mind make him an invaluable resource for this highly-specialized ministry.

Sanctification is God's part. But discipleship is us partnering with God to see life transformation take place. Through this book, I believe that you will be encouraged and empowered to take your church and ministries to next level of healing, empowerment, and discipleship.

May God's *shalom* be with you always.

—Rev Dominic Yeo
October 2019

Acknowledgments

THIS BOOK WOULD NOT have been possible without the help and support of many. First, I would like to thank my Lead Pastor, Rev Dominic Yeo for entrusting a group of pastors and me to develop and launch the DEW Ministry in Trinity Christian Center (TCC) in 2002. His support, guidance, and spiritual covering for DEW are what made it possible for me to complete this dissertation, now in book form, in the course of my studies in pursuit of the Doctor of Ministry in Leadership and Spiritual Formation at Portland Seminary. In addition, my heartfelt thanks to Apostle Naomi Dowdy, who has encouraged, supported and applauded me on since the beginning of the DEW Ministry.

I am also grateful to Rev Dr Wilson Teo, former President of TCA College, who introduced me to Portland Seminary and encouraged me to pursue my doctoral studies—thank you for believing in me. Two persons who helped me tremendously in gathering and sorting out the data are Angie Lim and Lee Kum Hing. They have most willingly given of their time. My thanks to all the pastors from the churches in Taiwan who participated in the interviews and all the pastors at TCC. Your participation in the written and group interviews was valuable towards the construction of grounded theory of this dissertation. My translators, Fook Neng and Sarah, helped me with the Mandarin written interviews and the recordings of the group interviews from Taiwan. A very special thank you to Dr Vincent Chua, who guided me in my field research and edited my first completed dissertation. I was referred to you for help, and you willingly gave your help without hesitation, seeing me through the whole process of writing. Rui Lin, thank you for the final editing of this dissertation and book manuscript, which really was a generous and diligent work, within a short space of time. Two other persons helped me greatly with the formatting of this dissertation—Dr Joseph Tan and Pastor Phebe Ngan (Thanks for the library books from

Acknowledgments

the National University of Singapore—did not forget). Finally Jessie Chew, you are such a great help—thank you for work of formatting to meet the requirements for publication.

I am really appreciative of all of my professors at the Portland Seminary. You have all contributed to my learning, growth, and writing of this dissertation. I am grateful to Dr Leah Payne, my dissertation advisor. You have been my most active and constant cheerleader—cheering me from the start to the finish line. It's hard for me to forget your exuberance, enthusiasm, and belief in my dissertation work and me. Dr Aida Ramos, thank you for the guidance on the grounded theory. It was your feedback that has given my dissertation field research the integrity that it needs. Because of your feedback, I learned so much more about the strength and integrity of the grounded theory research process. I am so grateful that Dr Mark Chironna got to read my dissertation and be on my oral defense. Your knowledge in the area of my dissertation gives me great confidence in my dissertation work. Dr Cliff Berger always attends to questions asked quickly. Heather Rainey, thanks for all the administrative support when requested. Dr Loren Kerns, you have taken such good care of my journey in this study at Portland Seminary. Thank you so much for your friendship and guidance.

I cannot forget to thank my DEW Ministry workers who have served with me in this ministry. It is because of them that I have this book and they have all prayed along with me. You have all cheered me on in my study pursuits and celebrated with me on my finishing it. Pastor Patsy Wong, thank you for your encouragements and ministry partnership.

And a big thank you to my wife Margaret and two daughters Hannah and Odelia for the companionship throughout this journey. It's great to have a wife who is reminding me of the important things to do and helping me stay focus on finishing my dissertation and book—not to forget your constant prayers to God for wisdom, resources, and strength to complete this work.

Never forgetting God, my Heavenly Father who has put me on this journey of ministry and learning. The journey began during my university years at the University of Windsor, Canada. At the end of a forty-day fast, the Lord gave me an insight into the inner healing ministry through the reading of Psalm 51 and an experience of healing from the Lord.

I started my inner healing journey by praying with friends. Later during my early ministry years in Canada, I was introduced to Wholeness Thru Christ Ministry and studied Spiritual Warfare and Deliverance with

Acknowledgments

Dr Roy Matheson at the Ontario Theological Seminary, where I graduated with my Masters in Theological Studies. Through many prophetic conferences, the prophecy would always be about bringing restoration to lives and the repairing of walls.

In 1992, TCC invited me to come on staff with them. My wife Margaret and I sought the Lord and had many confirmations on our return to Singapore. It was then that I asked the Lord why He was sending me there. His revelation was a mission to help establish the inner healing and deliverance for the church, as well as to bring the teaching and training into the seminary. In 2000, Lead Pastor Dominic Yeo sent me and two others to explore Ellel Ministry where we saw an inner healing and deliverance model that had a strong formal teaching component and a prayer counseling ministry component. The team returned to Singapore and created a inner healing and deliverance model for Trinity and birthed the DEW (Divine Exchange and Wholeness) Ministry in 2002.

In 2014, I embarked and completed a Doctor of Spiritual Formation and Leadership study with George Fox University. Looking back, I saw how God prepared the way for me to receive my doctorate. All the ministry work in Singapore and Taiwan became a wealth of asset for my field research. It has all been by His grace and His grace alone.

May this book be His voice of encouragement to his church to let Him bring wholeness to the lives of His sons and daughters, who will live to glorify His name and all the world might see His love, truth, goodness, and His saving grace.

List of Abbreviations

AG   *Assemblies of God*

AL   *Associate Leader*

CL   *Carecell Leader*

DEW   *Divine Exchange and Wholeness*

DVD   *Digital Versatile Disc*

EDT   *Evangelical Dictionary of Theology.* Edited by Walter A. Elwell. Grand Rapids: Baker, n.d.

IHD   *Inner Healing and Deliverance*

ISOM *International School of Ministry*

SL   *Section Leader*

SP   *Spiritual Parent*

TACT *Theological and Cultural Thinkers*

TCC   *Trinity Christian Centre*

Introduction

I HAVE WRITTEN THIS book to explain how Inner Healing and Deliverance (IHD) enhances the effectiveness of discipleship when it is included as an integral, essential component of the discipleship structure of a local church, contributing much to the spiritual growth and maturity of believers. By "integral" and "essential," I make the point that IHD is not merely a supplementary ministry, i.e., a "hospital unit" for emotionally wounded or spiritually oppressed believers. Rather, it exists as a ministry that is much more inclusive for everyone who wishes to receive biblical teaching on life issues and receive prayer counseling. Whilst discipleship has taken place with the present discipleship practices, there is a significant role that IHD plays in discipleship that has not been understood and implemented.

IHD brings a believer into an experiential encounter with God. This results in an effective and impactful removal and/or reduction of hindrances to spiritual growth not currently addressed by most conventional models of Christian discipleship. As the narrative in this research will show that an encounter with IHD will renew faith in God, impart biblical truths, and bring restoration and transformation to the lives of believers.

My research is supported by empirical data based on a unique model of discipleship (with IHD as an integral component) implemented in my local church, Trinity Christian Centre (henceforth known as TCC) in the island nation of Singapore. I also interviewed pastors from Taiwan who have adopted TCC's IHD model in their own discipleship structures.

Introduction

ABOUT TRINITY CHRISTIAN CENTRE

TCC is a carecell-based church comprising 7,500 congregants and 50 pastoral and ministerial staff. Some pastors provide leadership and pastoral care for the carecell-groups, while others specialize in overseeing the children, youth, creative, and IHD ministries. The church has a discipleship structure that trains Spiritual Parents (SP) to evangelize and nurture new believers, Carecell Leaders (CL) who lead carecell groups of about 12 people, and Section Leaders (SL) who oversee a group of four carecells or more.[1]

In addition, Trinity Academy is the formal equipping and empowerment arm that provides leadership training courses (i.e., SP, CL and SL Training), including bible courses, spiritual formation courses (e.g., Holy Spirit and I, Prayer, Identity-in-Christ, Prophetic Ministry and DEW Ministry), family related courses (e.g., marriage, parenting, communication), and life-skill courses (e.g., finances, tithing).

The IHD ministry in TCC is known as Divine Exchange and Wholeness Ministry (DEW), an integral part of the church discipleship structure. I am the pastor overseeing this ministry with a team of about 50 DEW workers who volunteer as prayer-counseling ministry workers. DEW has a discipleship-ministry program (that provides teaching and personal ministry) and a training program, that develops DEW workers into effective counselors. TCC also provides training and consultation to a variety of churches. Its global reach extends to many nations[2] who currently adopt our carecell-based discipleship church model.

BOOK OVERVIEW

Chapter One introduces the glaring absence of IHD in most local churches' discipleship structures. It introduces DEW model of IHD, one characterized by "events," "memories," "beliefs," "emotions," and "behaviors." Events precipitate memories, beliefs and emotions. The tagging of the latter (memories, beliefs, and emotions) with the former (events) depends on the nature of the events themselves, whether positive or negative. These combine

---

1. In June 2019, TCC's carecells transitioned into a new small group structure known as the "Connect Groups." The mechanics of this structure differ from what is mentioned here. However, these are immaterial to my discussion on IHD.

2. E.g., Taiwan, China, Vietnam, Japan, Indonesia, India, Bulgaria, England, Poland, South America, Thailand, Malaysia, and the United States.

Introduction

to produce mindsets that direct a person's behaviors, and ultimately, his/her entire life. This chapter also highlights the difficulties experienced by pastors in raising leaders who have themselves been saddled by past events, which again underscores the need for such a ministry.

Chapter Two examines data from extensive interviews conducted with pastors of seven churches in Taiwan who have adopted TCC's carecell-based church model and are currently implementing TCC's IHD model (i.e., DEW) as part of their discipleship model. Interviews were also conducted with pastors from TCC, the mainstay of the DEW ministry. The chapter also introduces a grounded IHD theory derived from the grounded theory method of data collection and analysis. It also showcases numerous examples of healings and deliverance and how these have transformed the lives of numerous believers. As these narratives illustrate, healing and deliverance are for today and not confined merely to the early ministry of Jesus Christ and the Apostles.

Chapter Three explores the biblical and theological connections of IHD to sanctification and discipleship. First, it makes the point that IHD is part of discipleship and sanctification for all believers, not something reserved for a problematic few. Second, it portrays God not as a transcendental, mythical or impersonal being but as transcendental and immanent who is ever-present, participating intimately in the lives of the believers by, for example, healing and cleansing them. I draw upon two specific biblical accounts (the washing of the disciples' feet by Jesus, the restoration of Peter in the book of John) as illustrative of the ontological omnipresence of Jesus in the Holy Spirit, who is the Spirit of Christ. Third, IHD is an important mode by which our participation with God and His involvement in our lives takes a reciprocal form. Our positional sanctification is but a starting point for progressive sanctification occurring in close partnership with the Holy Spirit.

Chapter Four examines church history with the view to understanding why IHD, at first prominent in the time of Jesus and the Apostles, sank into obscurity following the rise of secular and theological schools of thoughts, such as Aristotelian thought, scientism, and the cessationist and dispensationalist schools. The chapter covers the latter period of church history marked by the restoration of the ministries of IHD, with Pentecostal pastors and theologians increasingly prepared to consider the melding of spiritual elements with the modern world. The chapter shows why IHD ministries have historically been viewed as a "hospital unit" designated

Introduction

as "problematic, special and separate" from the rest of the discipleship structure.

Chapter Five explains the relevance of IHD in the context of modern society and provides guidelines for including IHD in the discipleship structure of the local church. It describes the postmodern worldview, one characterized by an emphasis on experiential reality, as opposed to the intellectual and disciplines-orientation of the earlier modern years. Importantly, the yearning for real experiences has created space for the insertion of IHD as relevant for a modern generation.

Finally, Chapter Six presents my conclusions that IHD is part of God's ongoing work of sanctification—unstoppable, though man had sought at different junctures to phase out the working of healing, signs, miracles, and wonders. Our partnering with the sanctification process through IHD is an integral part of the discipleship process of the church and essential for all believers—not just a special segment of them. Its relevance is for all times. Although the IHD ministry seems to have declined throughout large swathes of church history, God still showed His hand among those who were open and yearning for His presence and person.

1

The Need for Inner Healing and Deliverance (IHD) and the Definition of IHD

THE SPIRITUAL FORMATION OF a person towards maturity-in-Christ is often hindered by unattended emotional hurts, unresolved inner struggles, ungodly beliefs in their minds, spiritual oppressions, footholds, and other entrenchments. James A. Lang opines that some Christian leaders now recognize the importance of addressing the inner lives of Christians to overcome emotional roadblocks and deep-seated hurts in their lives, so that they may move on to maturity in Christ.[1] Seminary professor and Christian family therapist, Sandra Wilson, who herself experienced sexual abuse and abandonment issues as a child, testified that she had an awesome healing that she never thought possible. She admits that she had experienced growth in her Christian life as a result of Bible Study, prayer and counseling, but that these had not produced what she describes as an "unshakeable sense of belonging" to God she is now experiencing. Sandra describes her journey in life as an Evangelical, as one learning denominational doctrines, theological and biblical truths about God, but without the healing that has now freed her to have a growing intimate relationship with God.[2]

The discipleship structure in many churches lacks a ministry for the healing of hurts experienced by believers to varying degrees, depending

1. Lang, "Evaluation," 260.
2. Lang, "Evaluation," 260.

The Importance of IHD for Effective Discipleship

on their life's trajectory. The literature of several proponents on discipleship bears witness to this lack. In Dan Glover and Claudia Lavy's article entitled "Discipleship in the Real World," none of the six stages of disciple formation identified contains the need for ministering to the inner hurts, struggles, and spiritual oppression of a disciple.[3] Shirley Chris describes a framework for designing discipleship characterized by three main frames: paradigm, practice, and platform. These three frames comprehensively describe the purpose of discipleship (love God and love one another), the activities of discipleship, and the sphere of discipleship respectively. Whilst comprehensive, no mention is made of bringing God's healing to the inner hurts and struggles of the believer.[4]

Susanne Johnson charged that Christianity is seen simply as a knowledge of historical facts and logically derived truths from the bible about the ontological realities of our existence in relation to God. She says that: "One becomes a Christian by memorizing, and assenting to their truth."[5]

Finally, Matthew Meyer makes a comprehensive list of activities for developing Christian growth which include many practices of spiritual disciplines (prayer, fasting, studying and meditating on the Word, spiritual exercises of listening to God), soul-wining, serving, discovering and using spiritual gifts, and being involved in the community of believers.[6]

Again, no mention is made of IHD as a means to resolving struggles in the inner self of the believer. Such is the predominant discipleship structure of most churches—concentrating on "becoming a Christian by memorizing and assenting to their truth" (mentioned earlier by Susanne Johnson), but with little attention paid to inner healing.

In truth though, IHD is an essential, foundational part of discipleship that is often missing in the spiritual formation of a person's growth towards maturity in Christ. To reinforce this point, I will share four stories which are composites of typical struggles of discipleship arising from an absence of IHD in the structure of the local church. Some informants were unable to experience the abundance of life as promised by Jesus (John 10:10). Others felt unworthy to enter their calling to leadership and be effective witnesses for the gospel.[7] Some have also struggled with spiritual

---

3. Glover and Lavy, "Discipleship in the Real World," 11–13.
4. Shirley, "It Takes a Church," 220–22.
5. Johnson, "Christian Spiritual Formation," 315.
6. Meyer, "Practical Dimensions," 106.
7. Pseudonyms used to protect anonymity.

oppression hindering their intimacy with Jesus. Yet others have seen their growth towards maturity in Christ stymied by moral failure affecting their life, career, and ministry. As a result, many pastors and church leaders have found it difficult to raise leaders for the local church, despite having conducted many activities related to discipleship. I also recount the narratives of several Taiwanese pastors who were participants of IHD, and who had themselves encountered the love of God in a very personal way.[8]

HELEN'S STORY[9]

In 2002, I met Helen who was struggling with personal issues she felt she could handle on her own. She was, after all, a highly qualified consultant with a postgraduate degree. Her job required her to instruct managers in the areas of problem-solving and decision-making. She was a consultant to managers who had sought her help to solve their organizational problems. "I thought I was coping reasonably well", she shared. "I was reading the Bible regularly and was in church weekly. I even attended a nine-month part-time Bible course covering the books in the Old Testament; I even fasted." However, she was still far from seeing or experiencing Jesus' promise of abundant living. "I thought to myself, 'God, I've done enough. You've got to fix my problems, right?'"

At the time, she was going through a divorce and was experiencing a lot of pain, which she tried to drown by working late into the night or by playing computer games. When her daughter began having problems in school, the school counselor told Helen that her daughter had shared that she was negatively affected by her parents' divorce and had felt neglected. Realizing the urgency of the matter, Helen approached her pastor who recommended her for the DEW ministry.

At the first meeting, Helen's DEW worker sought a better understanding of her situation and assured Helen that it was normal to cry as a form of release. "In my heart, I was thinking, 'Oh no, this is not the way to deal with a problem. Am I doing the right thing? I can still quit from this.'" Then, her DEW worker suggested that Helen pray to declare Jesus as Lord of her spirit, mind, emotions, will, and body. To Helen's surprise, she could not

---

8. These pastors originate from different churches in different denominations, e.g., Baptist, Presbyterians, Bread of Life.

9. Helen is a member of my church, Trinity Christian Center. Her actual name is used with her permission.

The Importance of IHD for Effective Discipleship

open her mouth to pray. Instead, she started crying and was losing control of herself. Her DEW worker later told her to consider inner healing.

At the next meeting, Helen met with myself and another DEW worker who explained to her the process of the IHD ministry. She asked Helen for more information about her family, information that would be kept private and confidential among selected counselors only. Helen recounted: "What I want is to get my problem solved. What is the relevance of my family background?" Nevertheless, she yielded to the ministry and left the meeting that night with a big load off her chest. This first load was the pain, grief, and guilt she had felt concerning her mother's death. In subsequent meetings, she discarded other bondages and pains that came from past sins, the lack of forgiveness, hurts, unbelief, and fear.

At the time of this writing, Helen's situation has yet to change completely. However, she no longer struggles with the debilitating pain and bondages that had kept her from managing her problems and living life in the fullness of God's abundant grace. The beautiful closing words of Helen's testimony depict the beautiful inner healing work God has done in her: "At the final meeting, as the counselor prayed for me, I saw in front of me a bright blue sky with pretty clouds—Oh God it's so good to be free . . . through the healing I received from God, I am as free as I can be, and above all, I am able to grow and mature with the Lord . . . Jesus came that I might have life abundant."

JANE'S STORY[10]

Before she attended DEW ministry, Jane felt unworthy of entering her calling as an effective witness for the gospel. Her Carecell Leader had encouraged her to attend the Spiritual Parenting (SP) course and subsequently be appointed as an SP. Jane shared that she could not bring herself to do it. "I felt filthy and hypocritical if I prayed for someone when I was not clean myself. Although I knew Jesus had forgiven my sins, I still carried the burden of guilt and shame of my past which started affecting my relationship with my spouse, my children, my ability to love others, and even including my relationship with God." She said she struggled with memories of her past that she felt unable to share with anyone. She was molested when she was young, lost her virginity before marriage, and went through many failed relationships. All this made her feel dirty and unclean.

10. Pseudonym used to protect anonymity.

During the DEW ministry, the Lord released her guilt, shame, and pain. She says she now knows that not only have all her sins been forgiven, but the Lord has now dressed her in a new garment. Jane says she is now ready to take the next step to be an SP, to pursue God's destiny for her life, and to be His witness for the gospel.

MARY'S STORY[11]

Mary was a young Christian (of only two years), who loved Jesus but was struggling with spiritual oppression that hindered her intimacy with Him. Before she became a Christian, she had worshipped almost every idol of the traditional Chinese religion and had almost become a nun. When she heard the gospel of Jesus Christ, she realized that she had finally come to the truth of God's love for her and accepted Jesus as her Lord and personal Saviour.

Mary came for help because whenever she opened the Bible, she could not see the words on the page. However, when she closed it and opened the newspaper or any other publication (such as a magazine), she was able to see the words. She was attending church and carecell regularly, but her growth was hindered as she could not read the Bible. A blindness seemed to set in each time she attempted to read it.

During the ministry session, Mary was asked to stand. The moment she was prayed for, she collapsed onto the floor and started to speak gibberish. Her eyes turned upwards with only the whites of her eyes showing. I commanded the demonic spirits to release her. The gibberish stopped, and her eyes returned to normal. Mary stood up and was given the Bible to read. She was able to read every word after that!

SOME TAIWANESE PASTORS' TESTIMONIES

The testimonies below are from the pastors of several Taiwanese churches that had adopted the TCC discipleship carecell-based church model and had participated in this dissertation research.[12] An elaboration of their comments can be found in Chapter 2.

---

11. Pseudonym used to protect anonymity.

12. The churches were required to spend the first two years setting up the carecell structure, after which DEW was introduced into their discipleship structures.

The Importance of IHD for Effective Discipleship

"Before DEW was introduced to our church, we had members who knew nothing about the Holy Spirit working in their lives. They were serious Christians, passionate and wanting to serve but somehow they could not. After DEW ministry, their hearts opened to the work of the Holy Spirit and they were changed. They had experienced the Holy Spirit working in their lives, their hearts were submitted to God, and a change took place in their hearts. People experienced healing to different degrees, but there was a noticeable shift in the spiritual atmosphere of our church."

"Many co-workers were passionate about serving but felt stuck in their personal growth. They could not progress in ministry and had become discouraged. They were stuck because of past hurts and issues that were not resolved and the team could not move forward. Many tried hard to get breakthroughs through Bible reading and prayer, but experienced no real or significant breakthroughs. After DEW, they were able to let God lead them. They became confident in God and could partner with others to serve the Lord. DEW has proven to be a fast and effective way for recovery instead of just trying to do it on their own. It takes much longer when people try on their own through Bible reading and personal prayers."

"DEW is a great help to pastoral care and discipleship. DEW releases the believers from wrong belief systems so that they can begin to understand, assimilate, and align their thinking to biblical truths and God's purposes for their lives. This is an effective renewal of the mind, which is a great help to pastoral care and discipleship . . . we can now push forward."

"Without DEW, we were having difficulty pastoring and equipping believers to be disciples. They were struggling with serious problems with the powers of darkness: idolatry, divination, sorcery, adultery, and hurts of hearts, and many other issues. Many of them were struggling with bondages and temptations, spiritual oppression, and relationship issues, causing divisions. The growth of their spiritual life was slow and it was hard to achieve some level of maturity. After DEW was introduced in our church, many were healed and delivered. Many have been transformed into being healthy disciples of Jesus Christ."

Pastor C testified that DEW has helped raise Carecell Leaders for his church, which was difficult to achieve prior to DEW. Before DEW, leaders and church members faced many difficulties in their personal lives. These included family and marital problems, addictions, and other emotional and interpersonal relationship problems and hurts. He was not able to help them resolve their problems other than to provide pastoral care and praying for them. Although some did take up leadership positions, many could not persevere and lasted only a year or two at the most, as Carecell Leaders. After adding DEW to his church, he knew how to minister and help leaders obtain their healing from the Lord. He continued to help them, providing pastoral care, and nurturing their personal devotional life, in Bible reading, and other church involvement.

> "It became easier to raise leaders. We have since grown from less than ten Carecell Leaders to almost 40. There are about 15 Section Leaders from across the young adults and city districts. Among them, two leaders have become pastoral staff. There are four times more staff members than before . . . this ministry has helped us greatly in our work of expanding the church, pastoring, nurturing, and raising leaders because their lives have been transformed, their foundations restored, and their faith firmly rooted in God's truth."

WHAT IS INNER HEALING AND DELIVERANCE (IHD)?

Inner Healing and Deliverance consists of two separate ministries with two different but connected foci, with the same goal of bringing restoration to broken lives. The first ministry, Inner Healing, has to do with partnering with the Holy Spirit to bring healing to the emotional hurts and inner incongruences between thoughts and emotions, realignment to God (if there is misaligned thinking), and restoring mental orderliness. The second ministry, Deliverance, is the application of the delegated authority of Christ to the believer to break demonic bondages in a person's life that gives demonic spirits a foothold, including demonic oppressions.

Terry Wardle defines inner healing as ". . . a work of the Holy Spirit moving through caregivers to the broken and battered. The Holy Spirit uses these caregivers to identify root wounds, and to set people free from dysfunctional behaviors."[13] Wardle writes that the Holy Spirit disposes the lies that cause and keep people in torment emotionally, and sets those under demonic oppressions, free.[14] Here, Wardle connects emotional issues

---

13. Wardle, *Healing Care Healing Prayer*, 19.
14. Wardle, *Healing Care Healing Prayer*, 19.

with mental thoughts (lies), and demonic bondage. Wardle describes the caregiver's role as that of ministering the power of God through different methods such as praying with scriptures, healing prayers, facilitating encounters with Jesus, confronting sin and administering God's favor—all of which build the Kingdom of God in the life of the believer.[15] He asserts that both Caregivers and the receivers, in their encounter with Christ, are participating together as partners in the process of receiving inner healing, which involves appropriating Christ's victorious work in His death and resurrection for the restoration of human brokenness.[16]

John Loren Sandford and Mark Sandford explain that inner-healing should be called "prayer and counsel for sanctification and transformation . . ." The Sanfords explain that inner healing is about applying the completed work of Christ, both in His crucifixion and resurrection, and His blood, to every dimension of our lives that was not given over to the Lordship of Christ at the point of salvation.[17] The Sanfords explain that we have been rendered the status of perfection in Christ, but this needs to be actualized by making the work of Christ effective in every area of our lives through inner healing prayers and counseling.[18] They see an important aspect of inner-healing as identifying the practices of the old sinful nature that are found in the character of the believer, that have not yet been fully yielded to the cross.[19]

Charles Kraft, a practitioner of the ministry of inner healing, observes that the Sanfords see inner healing as aimed at "transforming the inner-being of a person, i.e. a ministry to the inner-person."[20] The Sanfords strongly advocate connecting the ministry of inner healing and deliverance together, when ministering to a person. It is the Sanfords' opinion that these two ministries must complement each other to make a wholesome ministry of restoration and healing, because each on its own, will not successfully bring about a wholesome, sanctificational healing and transforming work of the broken, towards a wholeness in Christ.[21]

---

15. Wardle, *Healing Care Healing Prayer*, 19.
16. Wardle, *Healing Care Healing Prayer*, 19.
17. Sandford and Sandford, *Deliverance and Inner Healing*, 22–23.
18. Sandford and Sandford, *Deliverance and Inner Healing*, 23.
19. Sandford and Sandford, *Deliverance and Inner Healing*, 23.
20. Kraft, *Deep Wounds Deep Healing*, 36.
21. Sandford and Sandford, *Deliverance and Inner Healing*, 25.

The Need for and Definition of IHD

Charles Kraft, further reports that David Seamands, a pioneer in the ministry of inner-healing, views inner healing as a type of Christian counseling and prayer, through which the Holy Spirit's power is released, to minister to some types of spiritual and emotional brokenness. He however cautions that this ministry should not be considered as the only right ministry of bringing restoration, lest it suffers the consequences of wrong expectations and applications.[22] Kraft offers his preferred definition, which converges with that provided by Betty Tapscott. This definition views inner healing as the healing of the inner being of the person (thoughts, feelings, remembrance of hurtful past, and dreams) through prayers that release us from bitterness, hatred, despair, guilt, shame, unworthiness, self-condemnation, etc.[23]

Kraft's own definition is that IHD is a healing ministry that is empowered by the Holy Spirit to render healing to the "total" person. He says that IHD ministry is targeted at the damaged emotional and spiritual arenas of a person's life, often disengaged and hidden in their memories, thereby necessitating a focused healing of even his memories.[24] Kraft's examples of human struggles relating to the hurtful events of the past include ". . . unforgiveness, anger, bitterness, rejection, low self-esteem, fear, worry, sexual issues, and the like."[25]

Kraft acknowledges the connection between inner-healing and deliverance. He says that the issues of spiritual and emotional problems that inner-healing attends to, are what give legal rights to demonic presence and footholds in a person's life.[26] Kraft's analogy is that ". . . demons are like rats" that are drawn to "garbage." He uses the term "garbage" to refer to the brokenness and hurts that demons lay hold of, as their valid reasons (referred to often as legal rights), to torment a person and to keep him in his damaged condition. These reasons or rights that demons use to build their strongholds, to torment and to oppress a person, need to be removed, so that the demons have no further basis to access that person or to remain, to torment him any longer. Inner healing is the process of letting the Holy

---

22. Kraft, *Deep Wounds Deep Healing*, 36.
23. Kraft, *Deep Wounds Deep Healing*, 37.
24. Kraft, *Deep Wounds Deep Healing*, 37.
25. Kraft, *Deep Wounds Deep Healing*, 37.
26. Kraft, *Deep Wounds Deep Healing*, 45.

The Importance of IHD for Effective Discipleship

Spirit do this job of removing these rights claimed by demons, and deliverance is the process of evicting the enemy.[27]

In this book, I address IHD as one ministry, not two. This is in line with Kraft's exposition on the issue of emotional and spiritual problems constituting legal rights for demonic attachments. Hence, if there exists demonic oppression of sorts, inner healing has to be administered, so that the demonic presence, control, and oppressions can be effectively evicted. Inner healing alone may not resolve a demonic oppression; deliverance is just as crucial. It is not true, of course, that every case has a demonic attachment. Some cases are strictly inner healing cases while others require both inner healing and deliverance.

It is important to reflect on several common ideas (and themes) that are in all various definitions of inner healing, inclusive of deliverance. First, it is the ministry of the Holy Spirit applying His guidance and power, through a believer in Christ, who helps another believer encounter the Holy Spirit Himself for his/her own healing, to the dysfunctional areas of his/her life. The Sandfords describe this as ". . . making salvation fully effective in all dimensions of our life and character."[28] Psalm 103:2-5 calls us to remember and appropriate the benefits of our salvation:

> Bless the Lord, O my soul, and forget none of His benefits; who pardons all your iniquities, who heals all your diseases, who redeems your life from the pit, who crowns you with love and compassion, who satisfies your years with good things, so that your youth is renewed like the eagle.

IHD is about appropriating, through the work and power of the Holy Spirit, the benefits of our salvation in the victory and work of Christ, upon our damaged lives, to experience healing, so that we can embrace the reality of our positional redemption in Christ.

Second, IHD is a work that involves the healing of our hurting memories, painful emotions, ungodly beliefs, and sinful behaviors. It is, decisively, a work that releases us from demonic footholds that keep us in bondage to sinful behavior, attachments which subject us to a dysfunctional Christian life, hindering transformation, growth and maturity into the image of Christ. The root issues of a dysfunctional Christian life include resentment, hatred, bitterness, rejection, unforgiveness, self-pity, depression, guilt, fear,

---

27. Kraft, *Deep Wounds Deep Healing*, 45.
28. Sandford and Sandford, *Deliverance and Inner Healing*, 23.

sorrow, hatred, feelings of inferiority, condemnation, or worthlessness. These are real dysfunctionalities (emanating from sin and brokenness) that result in sinful behaviors such as violence, aggression, anxiety issues, lust, addiction, and vengefulness. Once the root issues are tackled and resolved, there comes a change in the behavior of the person who now begins to reflect a wholeness in Christ. The person is thus submitted to, and aligned with the Holy Spirit.

Third, if there is any demonic attachment resulting in bondage or oppression, then evicting the demonic spirit is essential for there to be a release from the acts of sinful behaviors, and for real change to take place.

Fourth, the end and much-desired result is that the person is released from dysfunctions and brokenness, possible demonic bondage and oppressions, as well as from sinful behaviors. This frees him/her to respond to the continuous transformational work of growth by the Holy Spirit towards Christlikeness, to develop an intimate relationship with God, and to experience the abundant life Jesus promised.

Fifth, there is the building up of the person in truth from the Word of God during the time of ministry. God's love fills the heart of the person, giving rise to a desire for a renewed relationship with Christ. This gives him a new level of faith in God and a better understanding of his relationship to God the Father, who loves him. He also gains a better understanding of how to live the Christian life—the importance of forgiveness, confession, repentance, renunciation—and how these will help him remain free in Christ. These are the essences of IHD: discipleship takes place during the time of ministry through the examination, correction, and renewing of thoughts and emotions. The non-judgmental experience of DEW ministry builds confidence and trust in the continuous discipleship of local church leaders. Pastor C (Taiwan) observes that "discipleship is much easier because they (the church members) are more willing to obey and conform to the church's directions and goals. They realize that we are rebuilding them and it is to bless them."

THE DEW EXPLANATION OF IHD

The Divine Exchange and Wholeness (DEW) ministry was launched in TCC in 2002. I am currently the overseeing pastor for this ministry and was one among several other pastors involved in its design and formulation. The current DEW team includes counselors, a clinical psychologist,

The Importance of IHD for Effective Discipleship

two medical doctors, and many lay workers. The expertise of the medical professionals is sought (when needed) to assess the struggles, emotional, and mental conditions of counselees with specific issues and/or suspected mental disorders.

DEW equips counselors with an essential ministry skillset for restoring a person to "wholeness in Christ"—which is when a believer has experienced emotional/spiritual healings, is released from demonic bondages and footholds (if any), has renewed his mind to align with God's truth, has encountered God's love and identifies himself as a child of God loved by God, is no longer bounded by sinful behaviors of the past, has reconciled his relationships with others, has love for them, and is submitted to discipleship for further growth in Christ. The believer desires now to live according to the will of God, and actively pursues God's destiny for his life.

Changes in behavior represent one key indicator of restoration within a person. The diagrams below reflect a unique behavioral model of change. This is the DEW expression of IHD used by TCC. The diagrams are not copied from any prior behavioral models of change, but are based on a real-life understanding of DEW in the context of counseling and everyday life.

Our behaviors towards God, ourselves and others are often the result of (1) our emotions and (2) our belief system. Every event that happens in our lives produces a memory that comprises an emotion and a belief system (i.e., ideas, expectations, vows, values, philosophies, motivations, attitudes—how we think, and so on).

For example, a happy event will result in a happy memory. Good, healthy, and emotionally happy experiences produce a positive belief system attached to that memory, resulting in positive, healthy behaviors in the future.

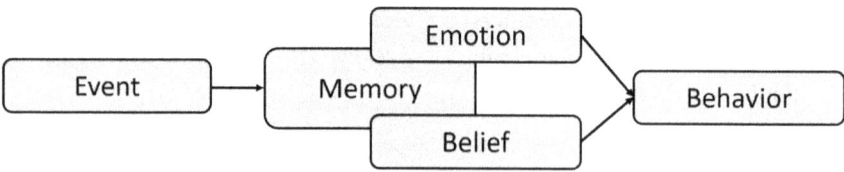

Diagram 1: Behavioral formation

Conversely, a hurtful event will result in a hurtful memory. Painful, negative, unhappy emotions and an unhealthy/ungodly belief system attached to it, produce negative, dysfunctional, sinful behaviors.

The Need for and Definition of IHD

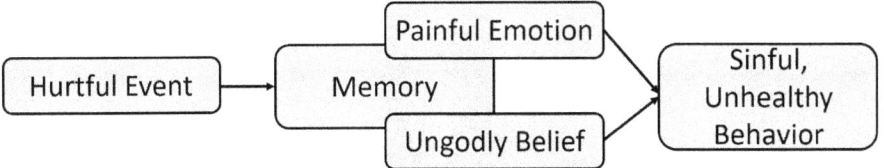

Diagram 2: Formation of sinful unhealthy behavior

An unresolved, hurtful memory will continue to produce ungodly beliefs and painful emotions that persist in keeping the person bounded to sinful unhealthy behavior.

Inner healing is about going to God with the hurtful memories, for healing of the painful emotions, and the removal of the belief system that is ungodly, thereby releasing the person to act in ways Christ desires. The ungodly beliefs are replaced by godly beliefs that are found in the Word of God. In addition, the person experiences godly emotions such as peace, joy, courage, love, and patience. This is the act of renewing the mind that Apostle Paul speaks about (Rom 12:2), often referred to as inner healing, which entails the healing of our cognition and emotions.

Under the DEW framework, discipleship happens in a real and transformational manner, with people encountering God's love. His healing and His Word transform their minds and realign their emotions and belief system to His truth. The believer experiences the reality of God.

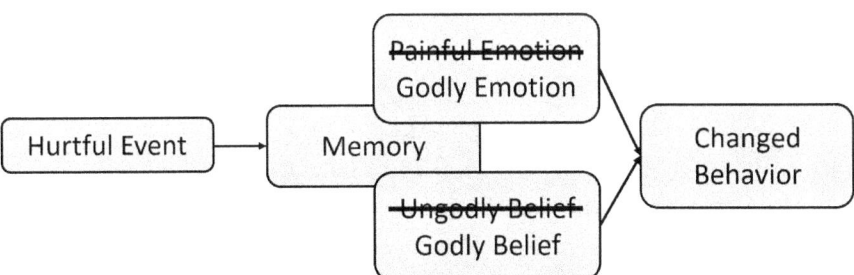

Diagram 3: Inner healing: Replacing ungodly beliefs and painful emotions

Sometimes, besides the ungodly belief and painful emotions keeping a person trapped in habitual sinful behaviors, a demonic spirit gets a foothold of his life because of sin. The demonic spirit keeps him bounded by ungodly beliefs and painful emotions, which coalesce and manifest in sinful behaviors.

The Importance of IHD for Effective Discipleship

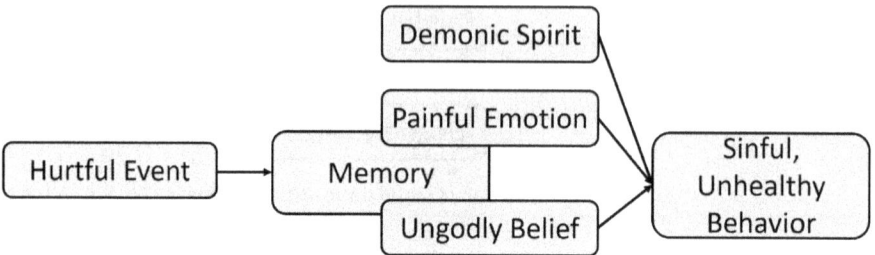

Diagram 4: Formation of sinful unhealthy behaviors involving demonic spirits

The good news is that God wants to destroy the work of the enemy—not just the painful emotions and wrong belief-systems, but also the enemy's direct foothold over the person's life (Eph 4:26-27). This is often referred to as the ministry of deliverance. Deliverance can be all-encompassing of inner healing, including being set free from demonic footholds. However, in this area of ministry, the specific word "deliverance" often refers to the act of setting a person free from entanglements with demonic spirits.

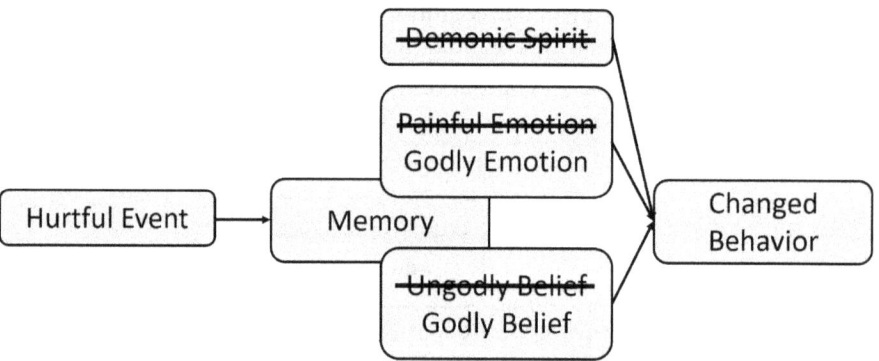

Diagram 5: Inner Healing and Deliverance (removing demonic footholds)

The result is the setting free of lives from impulsive and compulsive sinful behaviors, internal emotional turmoil, and demonic control. In addition to being set free, the ungodly, sinful belief system is replaced with truths from the Word of God, with the believer encountering God's love in a personal and real way.

Often, there is either a change in the behavior of the person, or his will is set free so that he can now be counseled further, discipled for growth and intimacy with God, and serve God's destiny for his life. Restoration of wholeness in the person is evidenced by his behavior of love towards

The Need for and Definition of IHD

God, others, and self. Discipleship has taken place because the believer has been taught what is godly and ungodly and has submitted himself to both healing and correction. In addition, he has had a real experience of God's presence and love. There is usually a deep sense of gratitude and a new level of faith in the love and goodness of God, that results in him pursuing an intimate relationship with God and serving God's will for his life. In the next chapter, I provide a more vivid picture of the significant impact that IHD renders towards effective discipleship.

2

Field Research

A Grounded Theory on IHD and Discipleship Effectiveness

RESEARCH PROBLEM

LITTLE ATTENTION HAS BEEN paid to the role of IHD as an essential component of discipleship in the context of the local church. Currently, discipleship processes in many local churches are centered on cognitive and behavioral educational development, hinging upon the dissemination of knowledge, understanding, and application via teaching and preaching mediums of instruction. Themes such as healing and deliverance are cursory at best, not yet integrated into the rest of the discipleship structure.

PURPOSE OF THE RESEARCH

The purpose of my research was to understand if and how the DEW model of IHD helps in the discipleship process: how it facilitates the freedom of the believer, and how it inspires the growth of the believer to be more like Jesus, set in the context of the local church. This research provides the methods and data necessary for framing a theory of healing and deliverance comprising the components of events, memories, emotions, belief systems, footholds, and behaviors.

Whereas most IHD ministries do not have a formal teaching program to accompany the prayer ministry for the believer, DEW is an IHD ministry with 15 of formal teaching accompanied by prayer counseling ministry. The teaching program touches upon topics such as: Reality-Check (reasons we struggle with certain emotional and sinful behavioral issues), the Lordship of Jesus, Acceptance of God, Authority of the Believer, Belief System and Irrational Behaviors, Rejection, Forgiveness, Godly Order in Our Sexuality, Generational Curses, Soul-Ties (occult and relationship issues), Accident and Trauma, and Walking Out Your Healing.

Theoretically (and practically), DEW educates the believer to know the ways of God (distinguished from ways that are not of God), and provides ministry to bring a person into an encounter with God. This facilitates the healing of their emotional wounds, releases them from spiritual oppression (e.g., from bondage to and from the past), and puts them on the road to freedom and realignment to God's will. Healing sets a stage for their subsequent growth into maturity in Christ. This book will propagate a model of IHD that promotes strengthening the discipleship structural processes of the local church, even as believers are walking into wholeness, in their respective life journeys.

FIELD RESEARCH DESIGN

Adopting the grounded theory approach

The research design presupposes an anticipatory and participatory research design (and worldview). This worldview has an action agenda for reformation. It is about advocating reform of local church discipleship processes to include the IHD ministry. It also hinges on a pragmatic worldview "that focuses on the outcomes of the research—the actions, situations, and consequences of the inquiry."[1] There is a concern with the application—"what works"—and offers solutions to the problem at hand. Thus, instead of a focus on methods per se, the important aspect of the research is the problem being studied, the questions asked about the phenomenon, and the answers that emerge from research and data.[2] In addition, I adopt a critical theory perspective that concerns enabling Christians to overcome the hindrances to the development of their Christian maturity caused by the deep-seated

---

1. Creswell, *Qualitative Inquiry*, 22.
2. Creswell, *Qualitative Inquiry*, 22.

issues of their past that continue to drive their actions and reactions in their life experiences.[3] Thus the end goal is to provoke considerations for the inclusion of IHD ministry with a formal teaching (and ministry) arm, to be included in the discipleship processes of local churches. Therefore the usefulness of the phenomenon (namely the DEW model of IHD) to discipleship is the main issue being interrogated.

The appropriate approach to this research is the grounded theory approach, defined as "a qualitative strategy in which the researcher derives a general, abstract theory of a process, action, or interaction grounded in the views of participants in a study."[4] Anselm Strauss and Juliet Corbin explained that the grounded theory is a theory derived and drawn strictly from the analytic work on a selected phenomenon. This theory is formulated based on verifiable data (related to the phenomenon) that has been systematically collected and examined. There is a congruency and clear relationship between data collection, analysis and theory formulation.[5]

There are four central inter-related properties that are observed in grounded theory, namely fit, understanding, generality, and control.[6] Barney G. Glasser and Anselm L. Strauss explained that these four inter-related properties basically ensure that the grounded theory derived is relevant (*fit*), easily understood by users (*understanding*), applicable to a variety of situations (*generality*), and allows users to continue to adapt it to changes (*control*) as time progresses.[7]

The research I have developed fits a large area of need in bringing wholeness to many believers' lives, so that they can be discipled towards growth. Pastors and leaders who are concerned about discipleship will easily identify with, and understand, the interpretive conclusions drawn from the data collected. The generality of this research can be seen in its applicability to the many struggles experienced by leaders and pastors when undertaking the work of discipleship. Finally, control is implicit in the fact that pastors and leaders are continuously a part of the IHD process, leading believers towards their healing; they are also constantly applying, possibly

---

3. Creswell, *Qualitative Inquiry*, 26.
4. Creswell, *Research Design*, 229.
5. Strauss and Corbin, *Basics of Qualitative Research*, 23.
6. Strauss and Corbin, *Basics of Qualitative Research*, 23.
7. Glasser and Strauss, *Discovery of Grounded Theory*, 237.

improvising, and thereby improving the process, as facilitators of the IHD process.[8]

Drawing intensively on personal narratives of life events, I began my data collection with the creation of four sample groups (this will be elaborated upon in greater depth in this chapter). Briefly, the first sample group comprised of pastors and leaders from TCC; the second of pastors and leaders from seven churches in Taiwan; while the third consisted of participants of the DEW model of IHD ministry from churches in both Singapore and Taiwan. The fourth group comprised of (and invoked) the written testimonies of some 843 past participants of DEW at TCC, collated over a three-year period from 2008-2011.

My research paid special attention to personal accounts and narratives, to better understand the experiences of participants undergoing DEW, adhering to the data-rich nature of grounded theory. The data (both quantitative and qualitative) are based on observations, testimonies, and interactions with participants.[9]

Subsequently, I studied the data and distributed the data into different groupings according to their common denominators through the process of qualitative coding. Coding is a process of labelling groups of data according to their identified issues.[10] The coding exercise began with open coding which sets the data into categories. Open coding is "the process of breaking down, examining, comparing, conceptualizing and categorizing the data."[11] The open codes are then connected through the process of axial coding. Axial coding is a formulated pattern of making connections between the different groupings of data so that a new perspective and meaningful interpretation of the data can happen.[12] Samples of my coding exercise are attached in Appendix A.

After completing the coding exercise, I examined the codings and created memos that underscored the real effects of DEW and the important components that determine its workings (including its success in transforming lives). Memos are "written records of analysis related to the

---

8. Charmaz, *Constructing Grounded Theory*, 2.
9. Charmaz, *Constructing Grounded Theory*, 3.
10. Charmaz, *Constructing Grounded Theory*, 3.
11. Strauss and Corbin, *Basics of Qualitative Research*, 61.
12. Strauss and Corbin, *Basics of Qualitative Research*, 96.

The Importance of IHD for Effective Discipleship

formulation of theory."[13] Samples of memos relating to Appendix A (Coding Exercise) can be found in Appendix B.

Next, I made comparisons of the memos and codings across all four groups of samples. This was important for discerning similarities and differences among the four groups, especially as the four groups are distinctive. The first sample group is made up of pastors and leaders from TCC (Singapore) distinct from the second sample group, which is made up of pastors from the seven churches in Taiwan. I conducted the interviews with the Taiwanese pastors during one of my missions ministry work trips there. The Taiwanese pastors and leaders agreed to meet with me in one location where I conducted three group interviews separately. I also met with individuals of the third sample group (from both Singapore and Taiwan), who had attended the DEW ministry on a personal basis. The last sample group was based on records of testimonies from some 843 past participants of DEW at TCC in the last three years. The interview data validates or invalidates the usefulness of the DEW model of IHD for discipleship. It also identifies benefits, weaknesses, and strengths. The data reveals new potential ways of improving the relevance of DEW to fit the discipleship process of the local church better.

Finally, the grounded theory used for this research was written based on systematically recorded memos and coded data. Although the research is primarily qualitative research, I incorporated some simple quantitative data to support the qualitative research, based on data collected from the fourth sample group.

Sample groups

The data collection of four sample groups came from the target population of many believers who participated in the entire program of the DEW prayer ministry (the central phenomenon of this research).[14] Individuals who had participated in this phenomenon, were invited to take part in this research. The first two sample groups (Groups 1 and 2) were designated as Category A participants, while the other two sample groups (Groups 3 and 4) were designated as Category B participants.

---

13. Strauss and Corbin, *Basics of Qualitative Research*, 197.
14. Creswell, *Qualitative Inquiry*, 120.

I applied purposive sampling to the selection of Category A participants.[15] I chose participants who were in a position to observe, assess, and comment on the impact of the DEW ministry on the overall church discipleship structure of the church. This was limited to pastors and leaders of the church.

Snowballing sampling was applied to Group 3 participants from Category B who were referred to me by the pastors.[16] These are participants who have undergone the DEW ministry, allowing me to ascertain the impact of DEW IHD. Convenience Sampling was applied to Group 4 participants from Category B, given the availability of testimonial documents filed with the DEW ministry.[17] Category A participants served to develop the research theory, while category B participants served to evaluate the theory derived from data collated from Category A participants.

Group 1 participants in Category A include pastors and ministerial staff from TCC. Eleven pastors and ministerial-staff (overseeing carecells) from TCC participated in the study. This group of pastors and ministerial-staff was chosen from a group of forty pastoral staff at TCC because they were most involved in nominating members of TCC to attend the DEW ministry. They were best acquainted with the DEW program at TCC among the forty pastors at TCC. The DEW program is an established program in TCC (operating for fourteen years now), and the participating pastors and ministerial staff are in a good and probably qualified, position to offer their understanding and critique of DEW as a discipleship process in the context of the local church that is TCC. A comparative analysis was conducted taking into account the views of different pastors and ministerial staff providing pastoral care, discipleship, and leadership to different groups of congregants within TCC.

Group 2 participants in Category A include nineteen pastors and ministerial staff from seven charismatic churches in Taiwan from various denominations (e.g., Baptist, Presbyterians, Bread of Life), that had adopted DEW in the past three to six years. The churches will be identified as Taiwan church A, B, C, D, E, F and G. These churches had adopted TCC's carecell-based discipleship model and had begun setting up carecell-based structure in the preceding two years. Subsequently, DEW was integrated into their discipleship structure. Hence the church leaders there are well

---

15. Chaturvedi, "Sampling Methods."
16. Stat Pac, "Survey Sampling Methods," para. 11.
17. Stat Pac, "Survey Sampling Methods," para. 8.

positioned to provide invaluable insight into the effectiveness of discipleship before and after (exposure to) DEW.

The two groups in Category A allow for a comparative analysis between Singapore and Taiwan, to determine if the usefulness of DEW is consistent in both contexts. If the results between the two groups are consistent, it will validate the usefulness of the DEW model of IHD to discipleship. Conversely, differences in results will grant insight into how variations between societies (e.g., cultural and other differences) affect IHD and discipleship.

Group 3 participants in Category B comprise 10 TCC and 10 Taiwanese believers who have been through the DEW program. This group will provide insight into the positive and negative experiences of DEW, having themselves undergone the DEW ministry. Hence, their accounts can be evaluated against observations among participants in Category A.

Group 4 participants in Category B comprise some 843 TCC participants of the DEW program over the last three years. 545 of the 843 TCC participants were women and 298 were men. In terms of their age, 152 participants were between 15 and 25 years old; 246 were between 26 and 35 years old; 241 were between 36 and 45 years old; 138 were between 46 and 55 years old; and 66 were above 55 years. Of the 843 TCC participants, 591 were working adults, 144 were students, and 108 were non-working adults.

The testimonies they have written are investigated to identify the value, improvements, and growth associated with DEW, and can be used as a basis to evaluate the observations of Category A. Since this was a simple quantitative study, no analyses differentiating gender groups, age groups or working/non-working/students were done. What can be said is that there was a fair spread of participant types—i.e. participants of different ages, men and women, working/non-working/students. The sample sizes of all groups in Category A and B (particularly from Group 4 of Category B) in this research, far exceed the minimum recommendation of twenty to thirty persons, by John W. Creswell.[18]

In addition, given that the study adopts an "anticipatory and participatory" and "pragmatic" worldview, the participants in Taiwan (i.e., church leaders) were invited to help design the questions; they were also involved in the data collection process and the analysis of information gained from the research.[19] The study has a strong evidence-based edge that advances the agenda for change and improvement in the lives of believers.

18. Creswell, *Qualitative Inquiry*, 121.
19. Creswell, *Research Design*, 9.

Research questions

Creswell, suggests that the research questions for conducting grounded theory should focus on discovering the individual's opinions of their experiences at different stages of their journey in the experience of the phenomenon. The initial documentation of the issues discovered should be revisited with the participants with more in-depth questions to facilitate a proper formulation of the axial-coding phase. He suggested that questions might include: What was the main concern about the phenomenon?; what were the reasons, conditions, and factors that created the phenomenon?; what were the different strategic plans used in the phenomenon?; what were the results and effects of the phenomenon?[20]

Based on the suggestions proffered by Creswell, two sets of research questions were designed. One set captured the responses of participants in Category A (i.e., both Group1 and Group 2 participants). Another set captured the responses of participants in Group 3 of category B. Data from Group 4 of category B include testimonies that have been collated over a three-year period of 2008-2011.

For Category A, an interview questionnaire was first administered to participants. The participants were asked information about their church and the discipleship programs conducted by their churches; the difficulties they encountered while discipling their members before sending them to DEW; the changes they observed in believers' lives after attending DEW; whether they were convinced that DEW is an important part of discipleship; and whether if there was no formal teaching program accompanying prayer ministry, would they still consider DEW as part of discipleship. A copy of the written interview questionnaire is attached in Appendix C.

Following the written interview, a group interview was conducted to gain better insight into the responses of the written interview. Key questions included: "How is DEW a part of the discipleship program of your local church?"; "If there is no formal teaching program accompanying the prayer ministry, is DEW still a significant link in the discipleship process of the local church?"; "What improvements or growth have you observed in believers under your pastoral care who have attended DEW?"; "Have there been cases with negative effects or cases of backsliding after attending DEW ministry?"; "What post-DEW follow-up strategies may help in the recovery of believers attending DEW?"

20. Creswell, *Research Design*, 66.

The Importance of IHD for Effective Discipleship

The goal was to rely on participants' views in the context of their life situations as much as possible. Interview questions were designed to explore how pastors and leaders experienced DEW as a discipleship mechanism of the local church. There were secondary questions asked alongside key questions, as the interviews progressed. Mostly open-ended questions were asked to allow the researcher a broad and general inquiry into the textured impact of DEW in the discipleship structure of the church. The research depended on the participants' view of their own progress. As active participants, they were well placed to express and give meaning to their growth process, set against their own unique social and biographical trajectories.

As in Category A, participants in Group 3 of Category B were sent an interview questionnaire with questions asking : how DEW has helped them grow as a Christian; the DEW topics that had helped them the most; the nature of their experiences with healing and freedom of the mind, emotions and will that have liberated them to pursue God; the kinds of hindrances to their Christian growth being removed; the nature of transformation, healing, change of perspective, release, strengthening their relationship with God and empowerment to faith and hope in God; how life has been different for them since DEW; the changes in their desire to grow into maturity in Christ and why. These questions were designed to understand (as well as chart) the path of healing, release, and freedom that participants experienced that has liberated them to grow as disciples. A sample of the questionnaire is attached in Appendix D.

Group 4 of Category B comprises a compilation of 843 testimonies of past DEW participants. Four types of benefits were explored. Type 1 probes the benefits relating to "removal of hindrances to spiritual growth." They comprise sub-themes such as: (1) being freed of negative thoughts; (2) emotional healing and forgiveness; (3) release from events of past hurts; (4) release from guilt, shame, and failure.

Type 2 pertains to the benefits relating to "positive growth in their personal life, relationships, and perspective." The sub-themes include: (1) personal life improvements; (2) relationship improvements; (3) the will to live; (4) healthy perspective of life; (5) experienced peace; and (6) regained hope.

Type 3 concerns the benefits relating to "Encountering God and Renewed Faith." The sub-themes include: (1) experienced encountering God's presence and love; (2) renewed faith in Christ; (3) growth in their intimacy with God; and (4) strengthening their identity in Christ.

Field Research

Type 4 includes the benefits relating to "increased motivation to serve God's plans and purposes." The sub-themes include: (1) renewed willingness to serve; and (2) commitment to pursue God's plans and purposes for their lives. The benefits were identified from the written testimonies and counted.

Two types of counting were conducted. The first counted the number of each sub-theme under each of the four types of benefits (refer to Appendix E). For example, under Type 1 ("Removal of Hindrances to Spiritual Growth") there were 453 indications of "being released from negative thoughts;" 573 counts of "emotional healing and forgiveness;" 594 indications of "release from events of past hurts;" and 303 counts of "release from guilt, shame, and failures."

Under Type 2 ("Positive Growth in Personal Life, Relationships and Perspective), there were 447 indications of "personal life improvements;" 262 counts of "relationship improvements;" 43 counts of "the will to live;" 186 indications of "a healthy perspective of life;" 240 counts of "experiencing peace;" and 160 indications of "regaining hope."

Under Type 3 ("Encountering God and Renewal of Faith"), there were 553 counts of "encountering God's presence and love;" 138 indications of "renewed faith in Christ;" 253 indications of "growth in intimacy with God;" and 313 indicated a "strengthening of their identity in Christ."

Under Type 4 ("Increased motivation to serve God's plans and purposes"), there were 50 counts of "renewed willingness to serve;" and 184 indicated "a commitment to pursue God's plans and purposes for their lives." The counts were based on clear indications of benefits accrued to DEW participants based on their testimonies.

In the second type of counting, I collated counts based on four general types of benefits. Each written testimony can only have one count of each category. For example, if Jane had under Type 1 (Removal of Hindrances to Spiritual Growth), one count of "release from negative-thoughts" and one indication of "emotional healing and forgiveness," the count for Type 1 would be one. If all four benefits under Type 1 were indicated, the count for Jane for Type 1 benefits would still be one. Each of the four types of benefits for the 843 testimonies were totaled and the results were as follows: Type 1 (Removal of Hindrances to Spiritual Growth) had a total of 738 counts; Type 2 (Positive Growth in Personal Life, Relationships, and Perspective) counted 616; Type 3 (Encountering God and Renewal of Faith) had 755 indications; Type 4 (Increased Motivation to Serve God's Plans and

Purposes) counted 221 indications. A sample of the counts can be found in Appendix F.

It is important that I interrogate my own positionality within the research. While I am personally (and experientially) convinced of the positive effects of DEW IHD in the context of discipleship, I must also maintain an objective stance. To properly assess the impact of DEW, I was equally vigilant about identifying any potentially negative effects of DEW IHD arising from participants' accounts. Thus I conducted my research taking both sides into account, the positive and the negative.

I am also aware of the nature of my ongoing associations with my interviewees, that is, the pastors, many of whom I already knew, were supportive of the DEW IHD. I, therefore, had to be especially careful in interpreting their narratives of the DEW process, not biasing a specific viewpoint to the exclusion of other viewpoints. During the interview process, I insisted on the interviewees being absolutely honest about their observations and assessments.

A GROUNDED IHD-DISCIPLESHIP EFFECTIVENESS THEORY

Discipleship process often reaches a stage of "stuckness" in spiritual growth

Discipleship is about transforming a believer to be more like Christ. Every believer has already been developed in a certain way (either positively or negatively), in this fallen world, before becoming a Christian. For some, there had been laid an ungodly foundation of worldly values and beliefs. Some would have received exposure to either good, or bad and hurtful experiences, while others may have been subjected to differing views of failures and victories, adopted good and/or sinful habitual behaviors, adopted worldly appetites, or even been involved in the occult. The believer would have had to walk out of these in order to enter and embrace Kingdom values and living. This is what discipleship essentially attempts to do.

While discipleship does happen effectively in churches without IHD as part of the discipleship structure, believers can often reach a stage of "stuckness" in spiritual growth. Here, disciplers are often unable to help believers make further progress in assimilating truth into their lives. Believers express this "stuckness" in various forms: being insecure about their relationship with God (e.g., not sure of what God thinks about them since they think that they are not good enough for God); being self-dependent rather than God-dependent; engaged in self-centered living rather than Kingdom-centered living; experiencing an inability to take up their spiritual authority to live life; in facing too many unresolved issues (e.g., personal hurts, failures and bondages) that impede their progress in the plans of God for their lives (they feel they have too many burdens to deal with; and have no capacity to be of any help to God or others); returning to past religious and spiritual practices; in lacking real interaction with the Holy Spirit and an inability to believe God and receive God's Word; in distrusting leadership's interest in their well-being and growth; and in seeing leadership as simply encouraging them to fulfill leadership plans for the church. As a result, they are unable to see or experience God's love or to relate to Him as a loving Father.

This hindrance to spiritual growth is exacerbated by the believer's refusal to commit to discipleship, claiming a lack of time. He also often refuses pastoral counseling, because of a lack of trust in leadership and has a lack of interest to grow spiritually (e.g., he holds little interest in reading God's Word and other spiritual disciplines). He is unable to see the root issues of his difficulties in experiencing breakthroughs and spiritual growth, and may end up living in denial, or simply being ignorant that there are personal issues of the past that are hindering his growth.

It is observed in this research that discipleship through educating the mind—via preaching, Bible study, personal devotion, Christian living classes, prophetic activation classes, and prayer—do often help believers, but only to a certain extent. These cognitive discipleship methods alone are often unable to be fully effective in helping believers grow in the image of Christ and in the will of God.

Pastor DY (Taiwan Church A) says that before DEW was introduced in his church, it was difficult to pastor and equip believers as they had serious problems, e.g., previous involvement with Chinese religious idol worship and Spiritism, or hurts from a broken heart. He describes his church as having had a very strong discipleship program before DEW. His church was a carecell-based church anchored on a "4 G" program: Welcome, Worship, Word, and Work. They later adopted the TCC carecell model, which includes a leadership development track involving the training of believers to become SPs, CLs, and SLs.

The Importance of IHD for Effective Discipleship

Although the church had special (and dedicated) teachings about worship, intercession, physical healing, counseling, prophetic ministry, marriage, family, Bible study, personal devotion, and an ISOM (International School of Ministry)-program for leaders (i.e., DVD Bible School for leaders), many believers in his church did not respond to the teaching. They did not grow, as they were struggling with bondages and oppressions from evil spirits and were contending with various temptations. In addition, people were often defensive in their attitudes and were easily offended, resulting in a discipleship process that was hard and slow. The pastors from other churches expressed similar struggles with discipleship as those observed by Pastor DY.

Pastor C's wife (Taiwan Church B) shared that they had many serious and passionate Christians in their church who wanted to serve but could not rise up to do so. She also said it was difficult to disciple the believers in the church because they carried too many burdens from the past, and were not sensitive enough to the Holy Spirit—"Before DEW, they knew nothing about the Holy Spirit in their lives because they did not have encounters with the Holy Spirit."

Pastor W (Taiwan Church C) shared that they had many co-workers who were passionate about serving and yet could not progress in ministry as they felt stuck in their personal growth and had become discouraged. She said they were stuck because of hurts from the past that were not resolved: "the team could not move forward." Pastor W also said many of the believers tried hard to get breakthroughs, but could not.

Pastor CBL (Taiwan Church D) shared that believers were often unable to break out of their bondages and had difficulties receiving breakthroughs to live godly lives. Often, leaders were unable to take up spiritual authority to fulfill the commission to save souls.

Based on the survey of pastors and Christian leaders both from Taiwan and TCC, the blockage appears to be bound up with unresolved issues of the past that include hurts from rejection, previous religious and spiritual involvements, relationship issues, shame and guilt, and others. These unresolved issues formed emotional blockages, reinforced wrong belief systems and other spiritual blockages that hindered believers from allowing God to do a deeper work of transformation in their lives.

DEW provides a process to help believers come out of their "stuckness," disrupting the ungodly foundations of their pre-believing past in order to facilitate transformational discipleship

A ministry staff from Pastor DY's church (Taiwan Church A) said, "Previously, I had been telling believers from my church again and again to the point I was exhausted . . . DEW is a great help and now we can push forward." She shared that DEW provided a means for believers to be released from a wrong belief system, releasing them to understand better, to assimilate and align their thinking to biblical truths and to God's purposes for their lives. She commented that DEW is a "great help to pastoral care and discipleship." Pastor W (Taiwan Church C) also shared the same observation. She said that DEW has proven to be a fast and effective way for recovery from emotional wounds, bondages, and strongholds.

Three testimonies from participants of Group 3 of Category B validate claims that DEW has helped believers tremendously toward progress in discipleship. A ministry staff from Pastor DY's church (Taiwan Church A) shared his personal testimony:

> "Before DEW, I could not assimilate or align myself with God's Word and therefore could not experience God's love. The Word of God and His love were locked out by the strongholds of wrong beliefs/false beliefs and ungodly emotions that held me from opening my heart to God's healing of my hurts . . . I used to keep reading God's Word but it could not build me up or change me."

Wu said it was the teaching and ministry he received from DEW that helped him. After DEW, he was released from the strongholds and was then able to receive the Word of God to build him up continually.

Li (Taiwan Church B) shared that she loved God very much and felt that God loved her very much too. She had wanted to do many things for the Lord, yet was unable to do so, as she felt a distance between her and God. She did not dare attempt anything for Him. She also felt that she was holding on tightly to things in her life, and that those things prevented her from getting close to God. After DEW, she testified that there was no longer any perceived distance between her and God and that she felt totally loved by Him. She also noticed she could let go of things. She perceived fewer obstacles blocking her and felt a deeper anchoring in God.

The Importance of IHD for Effective Discipleship

Zh (Taiwan Church C) shared that before DEW he led a very broken life. He hardly went to church, did not read the Bible or pray, and was easily hurt by others. Moreover, he did not have a passion to serve. After DEW, he was no longer as sensitive about things that used to hurt him, and knew now how to recover from hurts by praying for himself and by putting matters to rest with the Lord.

Pastor W (Taiwan Church C) commented: "DEW has proven to be a fast and effective way for recovery as believers are 'ministered to' as opposed to 'trying it on their own.' It often takes longer when one tries on his own, whether through Bible reading or through personal prayers."

Pastors of TCC shared similar testimonies of believers from TCC. Believer 1 overcame her issues of the past, became more open for discipleship and has grown tremendously since becoming a Carecell Leader. Believer 2 was able to identify her issues and trigger points. She submitted herself to discipleship and accountability until she got her breakthrough. Believer 3 forgave her ex-husband, received a revelation about God's acceptance and forgiveness, grew in the Lord, and is now serving happily in the children's ministry, fully integrated into church life. Believer 4 became an easier person to disciple. He learned how to be a godly man to his spouse and wooed her back. The marriage has improved tremendously and he has since become a Carecell Leader. Believer 5 was healed of rejection hurts. He experienced God's love and no longer sees his relationship with God in terms of "master and slave," or God as someone far away. His relationship with God is now more personal and intimate, like a "father and son" relationship. Believer 6 was healed of rejection hurts and has become more confident of herself. She is no longer stressed about what people think about her and has been learning to use Scriptures to overcome her situation. Believer 7 has overcomed issues of low self-identity, fear, and rejection. She is handling interpersonal relationships better and is now serving as a Carecell Leader. All these testimonies are significant evidence that DEW is an essential part of discipleship towards healing and wholeness.

It is significant to note, based on the testimonies of participants in Group 4 of Category B, that 738 of the 843 testimonies (87 percent) indicated a Type 1 benefit, that is, "Removal of hindrances to spiritual growth." Other Type 1 benefits include the following: 453 experienced being released from negative thoughts; 573 testified to being emotionally freed and forgiven; 593 were released from their past; 303 were freed from guilt, shame, and failure.

Field Research

A measurement of Type 2 benefit—"Positive Growth in Personal Life, Relationship, and Perspective"—is an important indicator of healing having taken place. This measures 616 of 843—seventy-three percent of all cases.

The DEW model of IHD, combining formal teaching and ministry, makes it a distinctive and essential discipleship component (instead of a "hospital unit") that value-adds to the discipleship structure of the church

Not all IHD ministries have extensive formal teaching on life issues to the degree DEW has. Many IHD ministries provide a methodology for doing the ministry with informal teachings on issues that are being addressed during the time of ministry. I posed the question to the pastors and leaders in Taiwan and TCC, whether they would consider as valuable, an IHD ministry without a formal teaching component. There were some variations in the answers of the pastors. All of the pastors surveyed agreed with Pastor A and Pastor B (TCC pastors), that some teaching is actually always interwoven with prayer ministry. Teaching happens during the time of prayer ministry as explanations are given to the counselee. In this way, teaching naturally co-exists with prayer ministry although it is confined to teaching that is specific only to the problem at hand.

Pastor C (TCC) offered the view that as long as teaching is involved, even if it takes place on a one-to-one basis during the prayer ministry session, discipleship can be said to have occurred. Pastor B (TCC) offered the view that ministry itself is discipleship because it is an act of releasing a person to grow in the likeness of Christ. Pastor D (TCC) pointed out that explanations during the prayer ministry actually constitute teaching although people may not see it as teaching in the strictest sense of the word. He added that this is because "human psyche-wise . . . we are trained to believe that we must sit down in a formal setting before we recognize it as teaching, and so, one-on-one prayer ministry is not regarded by many as teaching." He further pointed out that teaching during the prayer ministry session is very narrowly targeted at addressing issues that surface through the ministry time. It does not cover a wider scope of life issues that a formal teaching platform is better poised to facilitate. Hence in his view, discipleship does still occur when there is no formal teaching platform per se, but a more formal teaching program is often still necessary.

The Importance of IHD for Effective Discipleship

Sadly, it is noted that although IHD is recognized by many as absolutely crucial, it remains essentially an ad hoc "medical unit," or a counseling center (i.e., a service called upon only when the need arises). Its primary intent is therefore healing, and not discipleship. The potential of the IHD ministry to empower effective discipleship would not be fully realized in such an instance.

While it is acknowledged that some informal teaching and discipleship does occur during the time of ministry, all the pastors indicated a strong preference for an IHD ministry with a comprehensive formal teaching, covering the believer's identity and life issues. This is preferred as the most appropriate model. Pastor E (TCC) opined that "ministry alone is still part of discipleship because persons are dealing with their issues and encountering God, but a formal teaching and ministry structure sets DEW apart as holistic in its approach to discipleship." Pastor A (TCC) makes the following comments: "Prayer ministry is always accompanied by teaching even if it is very brief and not as systematic. My personal preference, however, is that some form of systematic formal teaching takes place so that the person receiving ministry is much better prepared." A lay leader (TCC), opined that formal teaching is needed so that participants are informed and will receive ministry meaningfully. Pastor C (TCC) commented:

> "Formal teaching makes a difference in four aspects. First, it helps the believer to identify roots of the problem and freedom is already being experienced before the prayer ministry begins (John 8:32—"the Truth will set you free"). Second, the formal teaching builds up faith to receive the prayer ministry. Third, it brings an awareness and a desire to receive healing. Finally, knowledge from the formal teaching keeps them free in the long run."

Pastor C (Taiwan Church B) shared an observation that before DEW, many in his church went through inner healing and prophetic ministries that had no foundational truth teaching. He noted that their lives did not improve. Instead they became proud and non-submissive, arrogant, quarrelsome, confronting the pastors and leaders. He attributes this to a lack of formal teaching (accompanying the prayer ministry), that gives a firm foundation in the Word of God, addressing spiritual and relational aspects of life, and promoting a sanctified lifestyle which helps people know how to live their lives better. Pastor W (Taiwan Church C) concurred, saying that without the formal teaching, prayer ministry can bring healing but cannot teach the person how to live a better life. Pastor C (Taiwan) likewise believed that formal teaching accompanying prayer ministry, helps people know how to live their lives better.

Pastor W (Taiwan) shared that in the past, before DEW, people who had gone for inner healing ministry became very ministry-dependent and demon-centered (i.e., always looking for deliverance from demons), and did not take personal ownership of their own growth. Whenever something went wrong, they would look for ministry; they relied too much on others when the responsibility should have been their own. She shared that formal teaching brings balance. Pastor C (Taiwan Church D) agreed with Pastor W. Pastor X (Taiwan Church D) said, that if there is no truth to align with, IHD would become merely a "feel good therapy." A good IHD program backed by formal teaching, melds knowledge with practical experience and inner healing. In this way, a culture of personal responsibility among believers is developed, which helps the church to grow as a whole.

These observations underscore the importance of an IHD ministry characterized by a formal teaching component, accompanied by prayer ministry. Although one can argue that some form of teaching occurs during the prayer ministry and that a person experiences some healing, the lack of systematic instructional teaching appears to create yet another set of problems for the leadership, such as an over-reliance on "feel good" emotions, without a solid grounding on God's Word, and the Truth.

The DEW model of IHD differs from many IHD ministries in that it provides formal teaching and ministry to resolve past entanglements with the world, and rebuild necessary foundations for growth and further discipleship. The formal teaching addresses the life of the whole person covering many key issues, all within the same period of time that the believer attends the DEW program. The formal teaching serves to identify the futility of a person's past beliefs and lifestyle, helps him to differentiate between truth and lies; breaks destructive mindsets; helps him to acknowledge sin; provokes attentiveness to issues requiring resolution with the help of God through ministry; corrects his understanding of God and his real identity in God/Christ; builds his faith in God; empowers him to take personal responsibility for transformation and growth; and establishes truth in God, enabling the building of a new godly foundation for growth.

Ministry facilitates encounters with the love, goodness, and power of God to bring emotional healing, releasing the person from past entanglements, canceling and rooting out ungodly beliefs, breaking him free from the bondages established by Satan and the world. The believer comes into agreement, alignment, and assimilation of the truth, thus removing ungodly belief systems and replacing them with godly belief systems. There is an intentional correction and reframing of the mind to God's truth and the reality of God as a loving Father, as well as a resolving of ungodly emotions associated with past hurts. Ministry also releases him to receive the acceptance and embrace of God the Father, which launches him into a new intimate relationship with God, in whom he can now fully trust and obey. He now becomes enthusiastic about living his life in right relationship with God and man, pursuing the purposes of God. The end result is a changed person who is enthusiastic about spiritual growth through discipleship; who builds strong, healthy, meaningful relationship with others; who serves God with gratitude; who lives a Christ-centered life guided by God's Kingdom values, beliefs, priorities and purposes; and who overcomes life's challenges through full dependence on the goodness of God.

The strength of a working partnership consisting of a formal teaching platform occurring in tandem with prayer ministry, lies in the synergy between the two. Pastor F (TCC) offers the following view:

> "Formal teaching brings clarity to right and wrong mindsets and brings truth to a person's life. Personal prayer ministry sessions are conducted in a safe and confidential environment, allowing for believers to be transparent about their struggles and issues. The openness facilitates an access-to-God encounters and healing experiences; it reveals the reality of who God is, and generates in the counselee a desire to pursue God and to be intimate with Him. Finally, the wholesomeness of the DEW ministry provides a new-found conviction to embrace God's purposes and destiny, and to walk in partnership with God."

Pastor C (Taiwan Church C) summarizes the benefits of combining truth teaching and prayer ministry in this way:

> "The teaching helps them to know that they can receive freedom through prayer-ministry. The prayer-ministry confirms the truth and provides for an encounter with the love of God and the benefits of the cross. I think that the prayer-ministry is to let the person experience the truth about God's love for the believer's life. Our purpose is to let the person experience God, bring restoration to a believer's life, and help him establish a relationship with God. To do this adequately requires a partnership between a formal-teaching platform and a prayer-ministry platform."

Pastor E (TCC) surmised the value of DEW in another way:

> "Believers have greater liberty because they become aware of their own personal issues and of how to deal with them. They have handles given to them through the teaching. There is an encounter with God and an acknowledgement of what God has done for them. Their prayer life improves. They have a greater faith to believe that God can change and transform their lives. Because they are freed from their personal issues, they are able to serve and have a greater capacity to serve."

Finally Pastor A (TCC) offers another important insight into the benefits of DEW:

> "The key advantage of DEW relates to the benefits associated with a concentrated and focused time of formal teaching and prayer ministry. There is an intensive and focused platform for many of life's issues to converge and take place over several consecutive days and sessions instead of the many aspects of life being received over the timeline of a Christian's life. During this intense, focused timeframe, key thoughts are replaced and aligned with God's truth, key healing takes place, and disciples are able to think, feel, speak, act and make choices to live a life pattern that is more consistent with God's will and ways."

In essence, DEW adds substantial value to the discipleship process. DEW creates in a person, a clean and healthy foundation for spiritual growth by removing hindrances to growth and sets in them, truths, both in knowledge, and in real experiential encounters with God's love and goodness. These inputs are achieved over a focused and intense period of ministry during which many life issues of Christian living are brought to the surface and addressed. It is like an old house totally demolished and its foundations immediately re-laid so that a new house can be raised. This is unlike a discipleship process with IHD ministry (but without a formal teaching component), in which people take a longer time to deal with issues in their lives. In the absence of a formal teaching component, it is like repairing or renovating different parts of the house and correcting different parts of the foundation, only as and when the flaws are discovered—as when someone falls ill and is only then admitted into a "hospital unit."

In the traditional IHD ministry (without a formal teaching program), although discipleship does happen, it largely remains only an ad hoc (or supplementary) ministry, and the church never fully reaps the full potential and benefits of it being an integrated part of the discipleship structure of the local church.

Discipleship-effectiveness improves because trust is built during DEW ministry. Participants receive help because of transparency

Pastor DY (Taiwan Church A) said that discipleship becomes much easier when believers are more willing to accept and conform to the church's teaching, directions, goals, and vision. Pastor D (Taiwan B) shared his experience that, "after DEW, hearts were opened, which is a major breakthrough. People had never been so open and willing to share about their lives before. This breakthrough facilitated healing in different areas of their lives. This resulted in a shift in the spiritual atmosphere of the church." In addition, Pastor DY commented that the believers realized that the leadership was rebuilding them via DEW, and accordingly, their trust in leadership increased significantly after DEW.

Pastor C (Taiwan Church D) also shared the same observation. He said DEW ministry builds trust through the sharing of personal lives. Pastor Y (Taiwan Church E) observed the same result among believers—that relationships of trust were being built (and restored), as believers became increasingly willing to share their personal lives with their prayer counselors. Moreover, the nurturing atmosphere of the ministry had touched the lives of many other believers in a deep way.

An important aspect of discipleship facilitated by DEW and being alluded to by comments from the pastors, relates to trust in the discipling relationship. Those who had attended DEW teaching and had received ministry, developed a greater trust toward their leaders that allowed for a deeper relationship. Pastor DY (Taiwan Church A) commented that: "trust has been built because they know that we are not trying to manipulate or control them."

Pastor C (Taiwan Church C) made the following comment:

> "Leaders who have gone through DEW training are also more open in sharing their own lives. In the past, we dared not talk about issues on sex. We could not open up so deeply and be transparent. But in DEW, we talk about everything and hide nothing. There isn't anything we can't talk about now. Thus, we can help

look after each other better, because we are more transparent with each other. As leaders, we feel safer."

Discipleship is at its best when there is open and honest sharing about struggles and issues believers face. DEW provides opportunities for transparency that set a foundation for addressing issues and resolving them with God, during ministry time. The extended benefits of this transparency during the time of ministry include the development of trust in the integrity of the discipleship process, resulting in growth and openness between leaders and members that make the discipleship process easier and more effective.

Discipleship made easier because of improved intimate personal relationship with God—the result of encountering God's reality during DEW

Pastor DY (Taiwan Church A) observed that believers began having a stronger personal relationship with God. Pastor C (Taiwan Church C) shared that after DEW, "many actually heard the voice of the Holy Spirit the next day. Those who previously could not see or hear anything from the Holy Spirit began to see, hear, receive, and see visions in the midst of ministering, and spiritual discernment was activated."

A few testimonies from participants of Group 3 (in Category B) verified the claims of Pastor DY and Pastor C. DEW participant A (Taiwan) shared: "After DEW, I began hearing God speak to me clearly the next day." DEW participant B (Taiwan) shared the same experience. He said that before DEW, "I was "blind" and could not hear God. After DEW, when the strongholds of the enemy were removed, I experienced God speaking to me through Bible verses during personal devotional reading of the Bible. I started hearing God's voice and seeing visions." He also felt very assured of God's love and protection, after DEW.

DEW participant C (Taiwan) revealed that she was a reserved person, who loved God very much, and who also felt God's love, albeit to a limited extent. She wanted to do more for the Lord but felt a distance between herself and God. Hence, she had not dared to venture into anything. She shared that she held onto many things that prevented her from getting closer to God. After DEW, she perceived a significant shift in her relationship with God, as she felt totally loved by God. She realized she could let go of things that once held her back. Her security was now fully anchored in God's abundant love.

Discipleship must facilitate the development of an intimate relationship with God. DEW participant A, B and C (Taiwan) testified to DEW facilitating this development, which the pastors also testified to as one key benefit of DEW. DEW facilitates a God-encounter experience that brings many participants into an intimate spiritual encounter with God, in a way they had not experienced before.

DEW participant D (Taiwan Church B) experienced spiritual renewal after rendering forgiveness, confession, and repentance of sin. There was a moment during the time of ministry where she encountered the Lord's light flooding her, and she felt His presence. She says her life has gone through a major renewal. It is God-encounter moments such as these, during times of DEW ministry that awakens a person's sensitivity to the reality of God. Therefore, DEW participants A, B, C, D have continued to grow in their personal relationships with God. Such outcomes are the work of discipleship facilitated by DEW.

Results from participants of Group 4 (Category B) reveal that 755 of 843 (89 percent) of the testimonies experienced Type 3 benefits, namely "Encounter with God and a Renewal of Faith." 553 participants experienced an encounter with God; 138 experienced a renewal of faith; 253 testified to greater intimacy in their relationship with God; 313 shared that there was a strengthening of their identity in Christ. All these attest to significant and compelling growth in their relationship with God.

Discipleship made easier through willingness of believers to serve after DEW

Another key area of discipleship is serving. This involves the willingness of believers to be equipped and mobilized for the work of ministry. Pastor C (Taiwan Church C) shared that before DEW, "it was impossible for us to lead our workers to a higher level of serving God , as they were so much filled with their past, which restricted them from living out their lives of service to others by using the gifts and anointing of the Holy Spirit." Pastor W (Taiwan Church C) testified that after DEW:

> "People were willing to serve because they had a deep sense of gratitude for the healing they had received from the Lord. There is now a pool of people who are willing to serve in various capacities.

We also saw more capable people stepping forward—it is as if their leadership qualities had hitherto been hidden by their personal problems. Those who had been serving before, became more effective in ministry. There is also stability and perseverance in their serving."

DEW participant E, a lay leader in the same church said: "Recently, we had one batch of people who completed DEW, and they all wanted to become Carecell Leaders!" He also shared that he had one member with great leadership potential who was resistant to becoming a Carecell Leader. Though he had availed himself to leadership, they found him difficult to work with. After DEW, his level of trust, obedience and commitment changed for the better.

Pastor DY (Taiwan Church A) said, before DEW, "we could only care for them. We had no ability to help them resolve their problems. Some leaders could persevere even with their problems, but others could not. Most leaders did not last more than two years." He continued: "After DEW, they were helped in resolving their problems and emotional issues—be it marital or personal. They also began to pursue an intimate relationship with God and learned to rely on God for help. We have grown from 10 to 40 leaders, with 15 Section Leaders and two Pastors."

Pastor DY (Taiwan Church) conducted a useful longitudinal tracking of the lives of six members within his church (this is found in Appendix G). Through the systematic collection of data, he found the key turning point of growth and transformation to be the introduction of DEW. Church discipleship without DEW helps mature believers, but only up to a certain level, as deeper issues in a believer's life would emerge and would have to be dealt with. DEW has provided the means for deeper access into believers' lives and has facilitated an encounter with God that resolves the deeper issues.

Pastor C (Taiwan Church C) stated that DEW is part of discipleship as it achieves the intent of discipleship. She defines discipleship as the transition and transformation of life from old to new, from believers to disciples, constructively shaping lives. DEW allows people to walk out of darkness into light, from brokenness into wellness, and into a life renewed in God. She also observes that DEW achieves another aspect of discipleship, which is that it equips a person to minister to others. Those who were trained as DEW workers are concurrently discipled to minister to others.

The Importance of IHD for Effective Discipleship

One result of DEW, according to Pastor C (Taiwan Church C) is that DEW releases a person to join the community so that he can now share in the work of the Great Commission. This is possible because a healed person can better interact with others and love them. Pastor W (Taiwan Church C) observed that after DEW, believers were better able to let God lead them; they also became more confident in their service to God and others.

A participant of Group 3 in Category B corroborates the valuable change precipitated by DEW. A sister (Taiwan) shares: "After DEW, I began hearing God speak to me the next day so clearly. I used to just go to church, but now I serve God passionately and God speaks to me. When I minister to people, the Holy Spirit just reveals things to me and I find it easier to minister to people."

Based on the results from participants of Group 4 (Category B), 221 of the 843 testimonies indicated that believers had a greater passion to serve and a greater passion to pursue the plans and purposes of God for their lives.

Some evidence of negative effects and backsliding after DEW

An important question was asked of both Taiwanese pastors and TCC pastors concerning negative experiences, or cases of backsliding after attending DEW. The Taiwanese pastors said that there had been a few such cases. Pastor C (Taiwan Church B) and his wife, said that they had only seen about five cases out of 100 who did not benefit from DEW. He cited one example of a sister-in-Christ, who was previously heavily involved in the occult. She was a priestess, had been sexually abused and raped, was intellectually challenged, and came from a very dysfunctional family. Although she received ministry, discipleship was still difficult after DEW. He also acknowledged that there was a group of believers who felt good after the ministry, but did not make progress after DEW, because they did not take ownership for their own personal growth in the Lord. Some other reasons for backsliding included being too busy with family, encountering unforeseen problems, not being able to resolve those problems, and not asking for help. He recounted some cases of people who fell back into their old patterns. He gave the example of a person who got worse because he refused to talk about his issues, would not let others help him, was still very defensive in nature, was difficult to follow up or dialogue with, was not involved in serving, and had a concept of God that was still not biblically based.

Pastor Y (Taiwan Church E) said there was a small number of such cases. The predominant reason was that they had returned to the same hostile environment that wounded them in the first place, resulting in much of the healing becoming undone. This highlighted the need for continued support and counseling to help believers discover strategies of coping within the hostile environments they find themselves in.

Other reasons for backsliding include believers attending DEW because they were coerced (i.e., not based on their own volition or desire), DEW workers' attitudes and lack of skills proficiency, and counselee's lack of faith, and poor perception of the ministry received. The believer's own lack of ownership was a contributing reason for the lack of success in some cases.

Pastors in TCC also acknowledged cases of negative setbacks. All pastors said these cases were, however, few in number. Pastor G (TCC) said she has seen about one to two percent of such cases. Pastor E (TCC) said she would give the estimate at around three to five percent. This was about the same estimate that most of the other pastors gave.

In addition to the reasons given, the Taiwanese pastors added that believers who were not open to the teaching, who wanted to continue in their lifestyle and habits of sin, who held on to pride and lacked humility, and who attended the program with an "I am okay" mentality, often backslided after DEW.

Pastor H (TCC) shared that most people she sent reported that DEW had impacted them very much. In the last five years, she has sent over a hundred believers through the DEW- program. Her estimate is that less than five percent of believers experienced negative setbacks.

Clearly, there is no foolproof program. While the ministry is effective, it remains up to the individual to decide whether to open himself to the ministry, and whether he takes ownership of his own personal growth after the program. Pastor D (TCC) opined:

> "Whether discipleship proves to be fully effective or not, depends entirely on the person himself. As far as the discipleship system and process are concerned, the provision for receiving ministry is made by DEW to ensure that effective discipleship can follow through, but the person himself has to take ownership."

The Importance of IHD for Effective Discipleship

Post-DEW follow-up strategies—TCC and Taiwan

It is important to look at the follow-up strategies to make sure that the links for continual discipleship is seamless and effective. Pastors and leaders from both Taiwanese and TCC samples were asked about post-DEW program follow up that would help consolidate the healing received and lay a foundation for continued discipleship. Sister I (TCC) reported that she had encountered difficulties in attempting to do follow up with some of those whom she had sent for DEW, as some believers were not willing to share about their areas of healing. Pastor B (TCC) said that she encountered similar situations. DEW provides a framework that could guide the carecells to help consolidate (i.e. close the loop on) the healing that had taken place during DEW. This would enable counselors and leaders to dialogue further with the DEW attendees without violating their confidentiality.

Pastor A (TCC) suggested that attendees be asked for their permission to share limited information about their areas of healing so that pastors can support their recovery. Other suggestions include the following: (1) getting them to revisit DEW to consolidate their understanding of the teaching previously received; (2) encouraging them to intentionally help a believer to develop his personal devotional disciplines of reading the Bible and praying; (3) helping them to continuously change and reinforce right belief-systems; (4) supporting them in meeting new challenges; (5) helping them develop new attitudes; (6) a mentoring and an accountability support system to reinforce the change of habits and lifestyle; (7) encouraging believers to attend "Intimacy with God" courses; (8) insisting on the removal of occult idols, relics, items, books, etc.; (9) urging them to live a greater commitment to carecell-life for regular nurture and care; (10) encouraging regular attendance at church services; and (11) inspiring them towards a more active life of s service.

Pastor DY (Taiwan Church A) recounted that some believers had been effectively helped by one-on-one, once a week sessions (for up to eight weeks) on reading the Bible and by being shown how to pray. Pastor C (Taiwan Church C) opined that follow-up review programs are important for believers' continued growth. She suggested that believers should be asked to come back for a review six months after attending DEW. This will give people a chance to affirm their God encounters and affirm how God is working in their lives. A participant (Taiwan) said having the believers testify in their carecell groups after the ministry, helped them to consolidate their encounters with God and their healing. In addition, he observed that believers fared better after DEW if they allowed themselves to be mentored for at least a few weeks (e.g., 21 days), to ensure that they were walking out their healing and freedom. Pastor F (TCC) suggested the creation of a recommended reading resource to help believers take ownership of their total recovery and growth post-DEW.

Admittedly, the general DEW framework does not have a post-DEW follow-up plan or guide for pastors and leaders to follow-up with every participant of DEW. However, TCC DEW has a follow-up plan of its own. In TCC, every participant is asked to return for a review of their recovery and healing process two to four months after they have received ministry. During this time, participants may receive further ministry in areas that need reinforcing and/or revisiting. Participants are also asked to reaffirm their encounter with the love of God and their healing by writing a testimony and a letter of thanks to the Lord.

Should the counselee be deemed (by the DEW workers) as needing additional help (e.g., accountability, counseling, extra pastoral care) after the ministry, DEW seeks the participant's permission to share relevant details with their pastors. This is based on the understanding that pastors are partners in the healing process of participants.

In the follow-up sessions, pastors meet with the participants to ascertain the kinds of pastoral care needed. With the need for a follow-up program in view, it is important now for DEW to elicit the suggestions of the pastors from TCC and Taiwan, on a suitable platform, as a way to close the loop on the IHD process.

CONCLUDING COMMENTS

A summary of observed results by the pastors of those who have attended DEW include character transformation, an ability to engage people, a willingness to grow in spiritual disciplines, a willingness to lead, faithful Christian service, a desire to share testimonies, a better understanding of God's love in a real and personal way, an understanding of their own issues, and an increased openness to share their struggles. They also seem more willing to be accountable and to receive intentional discipleship. All of these results attest to the value of discipleship having taken place as a result of attendance in DEW.

The Importance of IHD for Effective Discipleship

All the pastors in the survey preferred an IHD ministry that is much more integrated, as compared to one which is more separate in structure. An IHD ministry (with formal teaching and prayer ministry) was expressly preferred over one without a formal teaching structure.

3

Linking Sanctification, IHD, and Discipleship

IN THIS CHAPTER, I explore the biblical and theological connections to sanctification, IHD, and discipleship. There is an integral link between all three works that has not been considered sufficiently. This has denied the church of the inclusion of IHD as an integral part of the discipleship structure. As I will demonstrate, the research presented supports the integral and inextricable link between all three.

SANCTIFICATION

Definition of sanctification

As an ordained minister of the Assemblies of God (AG), I will begin with a descriptive summary of the AG's definition of Sanctification, as described in the AG fundamentals of faith. Sanctification is defined as "an act of separation from that which is evil" towards living out God's holiness in our lives, dedicating every moment of our lives to God (Rom 12:1,2; 1 Thess 5:23; Heb 13:12) This is in recognition of the scriptural teaching that we cannot see the Lord without living holy lives (Heb 12:14). Sanctification is actualized in the believer as he wholeheartedly embraces by faith, his identity in "Christ's death and resurrection." By faith, the believer responses to his relationship with Christ as a result of his union with Christ, by submitting all of his being to the guidance and work of the Holy Spirit in himself,

The Importance of IHD for Effective Discipleship

and by offering every faculty continually to the dominion of the Holy Spirit. (Rom 6:1-11; 6:13; 8:12; Gal 2:20; Phil 2:12-13; 1 Peter 1: 5)[1]

For the AG, the basic idea of sanctification is about being set apart or separated unto holiness. Sanctification occurs initially as a declaration that a person is holy immediately when the person receives Christ as Lord and Savior (1 Cor 1:30; 6:11). This means that the believer is separated from his past life of sin and is now dedicated to God. Sanctification then continues as "a progressive-lifelong process" of the work of the Holy Spirit, in separating the believer from evil and becoming more like Christ, drawing ever closer to God. The AG calls this the progressive aspect of sanctification.

Christians may not attain absolute perfection in this life, but we must diligently submit ourselves to the Holy Spirit's work in transforming us to live holy lives (2 Cor 3:18; Heb 12:14). Hence, the AG does not subscribe to the teaching that sanctification is a one-time experience in that a person is made perfect at the point of salvation. Neither does the AG embrace the Holiness Pentecostals Wesleyan distinction regarding initial and entire sanctification, which expands into a "three-stage Holiness Pentecostal *ordo salutis* salvation, entire sanctification and baptism of the Holy Spirit with endowment for power to bear witness."[2] Instead, the Assemblies of God embraces the finished work that "conversion came about because the sinful nature was crucified with Christ," and that "sanctification is a lifelong process of learning to live out once-and-for-all regenerated hearts."[3]

Other definitions of sanctification suggest very similar ideas. Henry Clarence Theissen adds "the imputation of Christ as our holiness" in his definition of sanctification.[4] Timothy P. Jenney believes that Millard J. Erickson's definition is the clearest representation of the Pentecostal understanding of sanctification to-date.[5] Erickson describes sanctification as a lifelong continuing process of God in making the believer actually holy ("holy" meaning "bearing an actual likeness to God.")[6] Sanctification brings the believer's moral condition into alignment with the believer's legal status of holiness-in-Christ before God. It begins in regeneration, at which a

---

1. Assemblies of God, "Fundamental Truth," point 9.—http://ag.org/Beliefs/Statment-of-Fundamental-Truth. Access July 23rd 2019
2. Yong and Anderson, *Renewing Christian Theology*, 108.
3. Yong and Anderson, *Renewing Christian Theology*, 107–8.
4. Thiessen, *Lectures in Systematic Theology*, 287.
5. Jenney, "Holy Spirit," 399.
6. Erickson, *Christian Theology*, 967.

person is born-again with a new capacity for a relationship with God. Sanctification is the application of the work of Jesus Christ to all dimensions of a believer's being.[7] Anthony A. Hoekema's definition of sanctification includes a call to a committed active engagement with the work of the Holy Spirit in transforming a believer's image and being into the likeness and image of God[8]

Comparing these various definitions, it is clear that sanctification is about a believer becoming more like Christ through the work of the Holy Spirit that happens over the lifetime of a Christian, beginning at the point of salvation, but continuing thereafter. At the point of salvation, the status of sanctification is imputed to the believer for him to have an intimate relationship with God. Sanctification then continues in the work of God over the lifetime of the believer, to enable him to grow into the image of Christ, but this requires the believer's own responsible response.

Sanctification begins with justification

Sanctification is the continuing of God's plan of salvation which began with our justification in and through Christ—without justification, there can be no sanctification. Before salvation, we are described as being alienated from God, "bounded in sin and death, guilt and estrangement, and ignorance of truth; bondage to habit and vice; fear of demons, of death, of life, of God, of hell; despair of self; alienation from others because of hurts and rejection; pressures of the world; a meaningless life lived in sin."[9] We were living our lives in opposition to God, perpetuating the rebelliousness against God that began from the sin of Adam in Genesis. Sanctification cannot happen without being reconciled to God. To be reconciled to God, requires our willingness to receive God's forgiveness given to us in and through the work of Christ that is provided for our justification. Neil Anderson and Robert L. Saucy say, "Justification is God's declaration of our righteousness or right standing with Him as the moral Law-Giver of the universe . . . Rom 3:21–26 makes clear this truth . . ."[10]

Rom 3:21–22 tells us that besides the righteousness of God seen in the Law of God, God has given Jesus Christ as another visible tangible form of

---

7. Erickson, *Christian Theology*, 968.
8. Hoekema, *Saved by Grace*, 192.
9. White, "Salvation," 968.
10. Anderson and Saucy, *Common Made Holy*, 65.

His righteousness, that agrees with the Law and Prophets, that brings those who believe in Jesus Christ into a right relationship with Him.[11] Verses 23–24 identify our depraved state of sin (our best state is still short of God's glory) that needs God's gift of righteousness through Jesus Christ to justify us. It is strictly God's gift of grace, meaning that there is nothing we can do to deserve His grace.[12] In verse 25, Paul makes it clear that this is God's work of propitiation for us through the work of Christ in His death for our sins, which is appropriated by us through faith in Jesus Christ.[13] The act of propitiation has everything to do with Christ bearing the penalty of the law in Man's place through His death on the cross (Gal 3:13) to make propitiation for our sins. In this act of sacrifice, Christ who was without sin personally, was representatively treated as a sinner and punished in the sinner's place (2 Cor 5:21).[14] For all who believe in the saving work of God through Jesus Christ, justification is effected, changing the believer's status with God.[15]

Daniel B. Pecota writes from a Pentecostal perspective that justification is about God declaring that a condemned sinner is released from every kind of accusation and judgement of sin and all eternal punishment for his sin, making him completely righteous (because he now has the righteousness of Christ) in God's sight. This is the result of having all of the penalty of sin paid for by Christ.[16] Pecota adds that justification is received by faith (Ephesians 2:8), although faith is not the reason for justification but the means by which we reach out to receive God's gift of salvation (cf. Galatians 3:6-9). He stresses that, "The New Testament never says that justification is *dia pistin*, 'on account of faith,' but always *dia pisteos*, 'through faith.'" [17]

Justification is God's act of declaring him righteous who believes in Christ. It is something declared of man but it does not make him righteous in his character.[18] Pecota explains that we do and will experience great benefits such as peace with God (Rom 5:1); preservation "from the wrath of God" (Rom 5:9); the promise of being glorified in eternity (Rom

---

11. Gaebelein, *Expositor's Bible Commentary*, 41.
12. Gaebelein, *Expositor's Bible Commentary*, 41.
13. Gaebelein, *Expositor's Bible Commentary*, 43–44.
14. Walter, *Evangelical Dictionary of Theology*, 596.
15. Horton, *Systematic Theology*, 365.
16. Horton, *Systematic Theology*, 365–66.
17. Horton, *Systematic Theology*, 366–67.
18. Thiessen, *Lectures in Systematic Theology*, 275.

8:30); released of all judgement and damnation now and in the future (Rom 8:33–34); and becoming sons and daughters, with an assured promise of life in eternity (Titus 3:7).[19] Adding to that is the presence of the Holy Spirit in our lives upon justification (Rom 8:15), who effects sanctification in us (1 Cor 6:11) and empowers us with His gifts to do the work of Christ (1 Cor 12:7–11).

Justification activates regeneration, setting sanctification in motion

Upon justification, God regenerates the new believer. The new believer is said to be "born again" (regenerated) as in John 3:3—"Truly, truly, I say to you, unless one is born again, he cannot see the kingdom of God." Being born again can also be translated as "being born from above." This regeneration is not about reformation, or becoming religious, or having a change of heart.[20] Guy P. Duffield and N.W. Van Cleave describe the new birth, not as removing something from a person, but rather as giving or putting into the person's being a divine nature that the person never had before, making him a born-again believer and a new creation in Christ. All this happens as a result of his submission to Christ as Lord of his life. "He who has the Son has life; he who does not have the Son of God does not have the life" (1 John 5:12; 2 Pet 1:4).[21]

It is the birthing of a new nature in the new believer by the Holy Spirit that has elements of cleansing—". . . but according to His mercy, by the washing of regeneration and renewing by the Holy Spirit" (Titus 3:5).[22] There is a birthing of a new creation—"Therefore if anyone is in Christ, he is a new creature; the old things passed away; behold new things have come" (2 Cor 5:17; Eph 2:10, 4:24; Gal 6:15).[23] The New Birth is further described as a resurrection in that the believer has been crucified with Christ and also raised together with Him (Rom 6:2-7).[24] Both truths are spiritual realities that come from the believer's identification with the death and resurrection

---

19. Horton, *Systematic Theology*, 367.
20. Duffield and Van Cleave, *Foundations of Pentecostal Theology*, 228–29.
21. Duffield and Van Cleave, *Foundations of Pentecostal Theology*, 229.
22. Duffield and Van Cleave, *Foundations of Pentecostal Theology*, 229.
23. Duffield and Van Cleave, *Foundations of Pentecostal Theology*, 229–30.
24. Duffield and Van Cleave, *Foundations of Pentecostal Theology*, 230.

of Jesus Christ.[25] The believer now has the spiritual life of God birthed and resident in him.

A very good description of this state of the regenerated man is that the sinner changes (Rom 3:9–18; 8:7) from a godless self-seeking lawless person into one who loves, trusts, repents of rebelliousness and unbelief, and seeks God's will for his life. The Holy Spirit has removed the blindness of the man to God's love, freeing him to discern God's love and truth and to embrace a life of obedience to God (1 Cor 2:14–15; 2 Cor 4:6; Col 3:10; Rom 6:14, 17–22; Phil 2:13).[26] The regenerate man is no longer the same person that he was. He is actually a new person in Christ because all of his past with its condemnation is buried with Christ and he is now raised in the righteousness of Christ to live a new life. (Rom 6:3–11; 2 Cor 5:17; Col 3:9–11)".[27] While this newness of nature and desire to pursue God exists, he is still very much influenced, and can still be deeply immersed, in his old mindsets, past hurts, and lifestyle practices, though he would want to break out of them. Charles M. Horne describes this old nature as "that capacity which all man have to serve and please Satan, sin, and self; whereas the new nature of the Spirit is that capacity to serve God, righteousness, and others."[28] With this new nature of the Spirit imparted to him, the believer begins his journey into the fullness of his being, and enters into his status of righteousness-in-Christ that God accorded to him through Christ's union with him. The journey of sanctification begins here from the point of justification and regeneration, with the impartation of initial sanctification continuing with the lifelong progressive aspect of sanctification.

Sanctification—the work of God as an initial position and a process

While regeneration is the point of the beginning of a new life at conversion, sanctification is the growth process through which the Holy Spirit brings the believer through into being transformed in the image of God, the likeness of Christ, in pursuit of God's will.[29] Though sanctification is a process, it begins at the point of conversion, simultaneously with justification

---

25. Duffield and Van Cleave, *Foundations of Pentecostal Theology*, 230.
26. Walter, *Evangelical Dictionary of Theology*, 924.
27. Walter, *Evangelical Dictionary of Theology*, 924.
28. Horne, *Salvation*, 80.
29. Walter, *Evangelical Dictionary of Theology*, 924.

and regeneration, because inherent in the act of sanctification is the starting point of the positional-status of being separated unto the Lord, and belonging to the Lord (1 Pet 2:9).[30] 1 Pet 2:9–10 states that positional status as a "chosen race, a royal priesthood, a holy nation, a people of God's own possession." A change of status has taken place the moment we accept His given mercy—once they were a disobedient people doomed for destruction but now they were chosen by God, who has made them a royal priesthood, a holy nation, a people of God—once they had not received mercy but now they have received mercy (1 Pet 2:8).

Duffield and Van Cleave explain it like this: "The moment a person is born again he is said to be sanctified (1 Cor 6:11)."[31] They call this the initial positional sanctification during which the Holiness of Jesus is imputed to the believer. The believer "may not yet be holy in his daily living, but the holiness of Jesus is put into his account, much like the righteousness of Jesus is put into his account when he is justified."[32]

Timothy P. Jenney explains Paul's teaching on instantaneous sanctification in 1 Cor 6:11: "And that is what some of you were. But you were washed, you were justified in the name of the Lord Jesus Christ and by the Spirit of our God . . . Paul says this work was accomplished by the Spirit (cf. 2 Thess 2:13)." The form of the Greek verbs "washed," "sanctified," and "justified" in this passage (aorist passive) gives no sense of any sort of process here. They all refer to the same instantaneous, completed experience: conversion.[33]

Jenney points out that while there is an initial instantaneous work of sanctification by the Holy Spirit, there is also a process of sanctification by the Holy Spirit. Horton says that the Holy Spirit continues His work with the believer in three additional ways: "(a) He continually sanctifies the believer from sin, (b) He increasingly delivers the believer from sin, and (c) He uses believers to assist in the work of sanctification."[34]

Sanctification begins as a crisis of status and continues as a process of God's dealing with man to bring him into a full realization of holiness

---

30. Duffield and Van Cleave, *Foundations of Pentecostal Theology*, 238.
31. Duffield and Van Cleave, *Foundations of Pentecostal Theology*, 238.
32. Duffield and Van Cleave, *Foundations of Pentecostal Theology*, 238.
33. Jenney, "Holy Spirit," 415.
34. Horton, *Systematic Theology*, 417.

The Importance of IHD for Effective Discipleship

that God intends for him in his being, character, and living.[35] Such was the experience of Jimmy:[36]

> "I was very burdened when I first came to church. Lots of anger in me and unforgiveness towards those who had hurt me in the past. I had lots of self-condemnation about things I had done in the past. My sexual sins were haunting me all the while. I held anger against my wife for her rejection of me as a husband. (This is the crisis of status that Jimmy was experiencing.)
>
> I have now reconnected with my wife and have forgiven my brother who has hurt me very badly in my growing up years. Thank God for setting me free from all this spiritual baggage which I had been carrying all these years. I have the confidence and faith that God is my Helper in all the circumstances of my life. (Through the process of ministry, Jimmy encountered God Who brought him into a realization of the holiness that God intends for him in his character, being, and living.)
>
> I have experienced restored relationship with my wife, my children, and my brother. There is also improved relationship with my co-worker. I have a deeper walk with God, and I have grown in my faith in God. Now I am trusting God more in every situation of my life." (Jimmy is now living out the life that God intends for him to live.)

This is a part of the progressive experience of God's work throughout the believer's Christian life of cleansing and purging from moral defilement and the building of the person into the likeness of Christ.[37] The apostle Paul says in Phil 1:6—"For I am confident of this very thing, that He who began a good work in you will perfect it until the day of Christ Jesus." Erickson says that: "sanctification is a supernatural work . . . done by God, not something we do ourselves . . . supernatural in the sense that it is a special, volitional work or series of works by the Holy Spirit . . . not just a matter of His general providence as universally manifested."[38] Theissen underlines the involvement of the triune God in the work of sanctification. He describes God's (the Father's) involvement in the work of sanctification as that of imparting Christ's righteousness and holiness to the person (1 Cor 1:30), and bringing correction to the believer to make that person become the image of Christ

---

35. Duffield and Van Cleave, *Foundations of Pentecostal Theology*, 238.
36. Pseudonym used to protect anonymity.
37. Duffield and Van Cleave, *Foundations of Pentecostal Theology*, 238.
38. Erickson, *Christian Theology*, 969.

(Heb 13:21; Heb 12:9f; 1 Peter 4:17f; 5:10). Christ's involvement is that of rendering His work (His death and resurrection) such that the sinner can be made righteous (Heb 10:10; 13:12), and making the person holy in Him by the presence and work of the Holy Spirit (Rom 8:13; Heb 2:11). The Holy Spirit works to free the believer from his depraved nature (Rom 8:2) by helping the believer put to death the old self as in being crucified with Christ, and in being buried in His death (Rom 8:13), and producing growth in the fruit of the Spirit (Gal 4:22ff).[39]

Thiessen while pointing out the involvement of the triune God in sanctification, also states that the immediate work with the believer is done by the Holy Spirit. While the formation of the Christlikeness in us is the work of the Holy Spirit, Paul underscores the need for our active partnership with the Holy Spirit, so that He can perform the work of sanctification in us.

Paul on our partnership with God

Sanctification is the work of the Holy Spirit in our lives and it requires our partnership. Theissen explains that both God and man are involved in God's sanctification work of man.[40] Paul writes in Philippians: "Work out your salvation with fear and trembling; for God is at work in you, both to will and to work for His good pleasure (Phil 2:12–13)." Rom 8:13 says: ". . . for if you are living according to the flesh, you must die; but if by the Spirit you are putting to death the deeds of the body, you will live."

Erickson points out that a believer has a responsible commitment to be actively involved in God's work of sanctification involving both the eradication of sin in our whole being (thoughts, emotions and actions), and our growth towards the image of Christ."[41] Paul tells the Corinthian church: "Let us cleanse ourselves from all defilement of the flesh and spirit, perfecting holiness in the fear of God (2 Cor 7:1)." In Rom 12:2, Paul says: "And do not be conformed to this world, but be transformed by the renewing of your mind, so that you may prove what the will of God is, that which is good and acceptable and perfect." In other words, Paul is saying that we have an active role to play in partnering with God in His sanctification of our lives.

39. Thiessen, *Lectures in Systematic Theology*, 292.
40. Thiessen, *Lectures in Systematic Theology*, 292.
41. Erickson, *Christian Theology*, 971.

The Importance of IHD for Effective Discipleship

William W. Menzies and Stanley M. Horton agree that both God and man are involved in man's sanctification. Their position is that it is the believer's role to actively partner with God, in the fight against sin, and to embrace the God given side of sanctification. However they believe that it is God who takes total responsibility for progressively working with us in the work of sanctification. The Holy Spirit works at cleansing us to bring us into alignment with how to live godly lives in obedience to God's truth. The believer's responsibility is to diligently respond to God's work in putting to death all thoughts, emotions and behavioral actions that are ungodly in all areas of our lives, addressing issues that include depraved human sexuality, ungodly deviances, wickedness, ungodly wants, and envy (Col 3:5).[42]

In 2 Tim 2:15, Paul tells the church "Be diligent to present yourself approved to God as a workman who does not need to be ashamed, accurately handling the word of truth." He then tells them to do this by cleansing themselves of, abstaining from, and fleeing from wickedness that dishonors God, and instead to pursue righteousness, faith, love, and peace from a pure heart (verses 19–22). Paul says that "the Lord knows those who are His" (verse 19)—those who cleanse themselves and are in pursuit of righteousness, faith, love, and peace, and calls on the Lord with a pure heart (verses 21–22).

With reference to the understanding of IHD laid out in Chapter 1, IHD ministry is akin to the involvement of believers in partnership with the Holy Spirit in the act of cleansing themselves—"Therefore, if anyone cleanses himself from these things, he will be a vessel of honor, sanctified, useful to the Master, prepared for every good work." (2 Tim 2:21) IHD is akin to Paul's instruction and is, therefore, a God-given means of sanctification in which we are partnering with God in the process, taking responsibility in cleansing ourselves by submission to the Holy Spirit's work. The IHD ministry has two parts in its prayer ministry. First, there is the act of breaking the believer free from ungodly thoughts, sins, and ungodly spiritual footholds, followed by the act of building up the believer in the truth of God through prayer. There is a clear act of "putting aside" (verse 8) and "putting on" (verses 9,12,14) that Paul instructs the church to do in Col 3:5–10, both important parts of the cleansing process referred to in 2 Tim 2:21. Mary[43] testified:

---

42. Menzies and Horton, *Bible Doctrines*, 152.
43. Pseudonym used to protect anonymity.

Linking Sanctification, IHD, and Discipleship

> "I literally looked forward to the DEW sessions. At each session, I emptied myself of all the junk and went home cleaner and feeling better. All the confession, repentance, and forgiveness enabled me to be more sensitive to the Holy Spirit's guidance. Through the sessions, the building in of God's Word also ministered to me. After the last session, I fasted for two weeks. I thank God for enabling me to draw near to Him again, and for rebuilding my relationship with Father God. I prayed and committed myself to be a living sacrifice for the Lord."

DEW accomplishes this cleansing process in both the formal teaching component of the ministry alongside the prayer ministry component. The formal teaching component helps the counselees to identify godly and ungodly principles and activities, while the prayer ministry component allows the counselees to submit themselves to the Holy Spirit's work of "putting off" or "getting rid" of ungodly sinful issues, followed by "putting on" or "building in" God's truth and principles of godly living through prayer. This is the cleansing work of IHD that is a part of the sanctification process. James[44] testifies:

> "Through DEW, I understood many things that helped me grow in my walk with God, and in my marriage. I understood the concept of spiritual authority, and that has helped me tremendously. During consecutive visits to Melaka, I was "challenged" by the enemy but the knowledge I had gained helped me to cast him out. Another thing was the possibility of the presence of generational curses that may have contributed to my sexual iniquities. Although I take full responsibility for my sins, knowing this helped me recognize and be aware of the enemy's lies and helped me deal with my sexual iniquities effectively, through prayer.
>
> Since the DEW weekend, I have not had major issues with lust and no longer have the desire nor experience the temptation, to go back to my sinful past. My relationship with my wife has improved tremendously. DEW has also helped me in my walk with God!"

Jesus on our partnership with God

Jesus told His disciples that they needed to be involved in His work of cleansing their lives and each other's lives so that they belong to Him. In the episode of Jesus washing the feet of His disciples, the main purpose

---

44. Pseudonym used to protect anonymity.

The Importance of IHD for Effective Discipleship

was about belonging to Him, and about becoming who He is, through and in them. John records this episode of feet washing in John 13:1–17. At the feast of the Passover, Jesus got up from the supper, laid his garments aside and took a towel and wrapped it around his waist (verse 3). He then proceeded to pour water into a basin and began to wash his disciples' feet and to wipe them dry.

Peter refused to let Jesus wash his feet because he felt indignant that the master should lower himself to the status of a slave to wash a disciple's feet. To Peter, this is not the respectable task of his master, Jesus Christ, but that was not the issue. Jesus told Peter in verse 7 that he had missed the meaning of what He was doing in the act of washing his feet—"What I do you do not realize now, but you will understand hereafter." Peter still refused in verse 8—"Never shall you wash my feet!"

It is at this point that Jesus states His purpose of washing His disciple's feet in verse 8—"If I do not wash you, you have no part with Me." Jesus says that the importance of what He was doing for them was to enable them to be a part of Him. It is about belonging to Him and becoming like Him. This act of Jesus washing their feet has to do with their transformation into the likeness of Christ. Peter, on hearing that this act has to do with being a part of Jesus, immediately responds in verse 9, with what looks like a total submission to Jesus, to gain total acceptance—"Lord, then wash not only my feet, but also my hands and my head."

Jesus' reply in verse 10, is that whoever has had a bath is already clean but still needs to have his feet washed—"He who has bathed needs only to wash his feet, but is completely clean; and you are all clean, but not all of you," In other words, the believer who accepts Jesus as Lord and Master already has a clean status with God and is accepted by God. The believer has an initial positional status with God the moment he believes.

Therefore, the issue is not acceptance or having a clean status (*that* is already settled), but the formation of the likeness of Christ in us. It is about a cleansing act that must happen continuously so that the clean status that we received from God (because we believe in Christ's work for us), is realized in us every moment, on the way to our becoming the likeness of Christ in our being and doing. This is the reason the Lord said only the feet needs to be washed.

When we have taken a bath, it is our feet that continue to encounter the dirt on the ground and they become dirty again and again, even though our body is clean. The feet are the parts of the body that come into contact

Linking Sanctification, IHD, and Discipleship

with the roughness of the floor, that suffer abrasion and injury, that touch the dirt on the floor and become in turn dirtied by it. Therefore, cleaning and healing are always needed. It is so much like the life we live: we are continuously buffeted by events and injured by others. Sometimes, we react in sinful thoughts and behaviors that do not resemble Christ or the righteousness of God. Besides being hurt by others, we also struggle daily with temptations and challenges that draw us to respond outside of our Christian character, forming in us another person outside the character of Christ. Hence, we need to let God continuously "clean" our lives—"wash our feet"—and restore our being in Christ so that we truly belong to Him. The washing of feet is an analogical parabolic teaching of Christ that points to the continuous work of sanctification that Jesus needs to do for us, so that we belong to Him. In Paul's words, it is the act of "putting off" and "putting on" (Eph 4:22, 24).[45] It is the act of renewing the mind, it is the act of cleaning the house out of things that are dishonoring to God; it is not letting the devil get a foothold in our lives (Eph 4:26–27). It is the work of sanctification that must continue all throughout the Christian life.

Cheryl Bridges Johns referred to foot washing as "Cleansing on the Journey."[46] She says that this act of washing of feet is an act of penance—a confession of the brokenness and sinfulness that we as believers continue to gather in our life journey, and our constant need for grace, forgiveness and healing from God that comes with someone washing our feet.[47]

She alludes to the need for cleansing in our journey as Christians; she also addresses the role of believers as agents of foot washing. The participant who washes the feet is God's agent of grace, mercy, cleansing and healing for the recipient who suffers from the pains of being hurt. This is the act that demonstrates tangibly the presence of God, His power and His grace to all man through the community of the believers—the church, the priesthood of believers.[48]

Bridges Johns takes foot washing strictly as a ritual to be performed. However, what is important is the intent or purpose of foot washing and the principle of foot washing. The intent of foot washing is that we might belong to Jesus. It is about Christ calling us to participate with Him in helping each other grow in Him, as we go through the challenges of life.

---

45. Horne, *Salvation*, 80.
46. Mannoia and Thorsen, *Holiness Manifesto*, 159.
47. Mannoia and Thorsen, *Holiness Manifesto*, 159.
48. Mannoia and Thorsen, *Holiness Manifesto*, 159.

The Importance of IHD for Effective Discipleship

What is important to note and understand in this whole teaching episode is that there were two roles that the disciples were called to be involved in. First, as recipients to let someone wash their feet for them. Jesus said to Peter in verse 8: "If I do not wash you, you have to no part with Me." In other words, Peter needed to be a recipient of the act of foot washing by Jesus. Second, Jesus asked His disciples to partner with Him to wash the feet of each other. In verses 12-15, Jesus said to His disciples: "Do you know what I have done for you? You call Me Teacher and Lord; and you are right, for so I am. If I then, the Lord and Teacher, washed your feet, you also ought to wash one another's feet. For I gave you an example that you also should do as I did to you." He would no longer be with them physically to teach them, to correct them, and to empower them. This was the last supper that He would have with them before the crucifixion, the resurrection, and the ascension.

The disciples would now have to help each other grow in the likeness of Christ in their being and doing, through the guidance of the Holy Spirit that was sent by Jesus at the time of Pentecost. Jesus said in verse 17 that they would all be blessed if they do this (washing each other's feet)—"If you know these things, you are blessed if you do it." Although sanctification can only be accomplished by the Holy Spirit, we are asked to take an active role in being a recipient and a foot-washer. The call to be involved in washing the feet of someone is a definitive instruction, not merely a suggestion.

Theissen affirms man's participation in the work of sanctification. He says that after the first step of exercising his faith in Christ in becoming a believer, the believer is sanctified positionally because Christ is in him (1 Cor 1:30). But after that, comes his responsibility to pursue holiness. Theissen says that the man who does not actively participate in sanctification will not see God (2 Cor 7:1; Heb 12:14). The believer pursues sanctification by yielding to God's act of exposing the wickedness of the heart, and his failures in holy living, and God makes the remedy as the believer surrenders to Him. Surrendering our lives to God is a necessary condition for effective participation in God's work of sanctification (Rom 6:13, 19–21; 12:1f; 2 Tim 2:21). The heart of God desires holiness for all of His believers because He is holy. God is able to accomplish this only when the believers yield to His formation of them to become like Christ.[49]

At salvation, the initial positional status of sanctification, the righteousness and holiness of Christ, is imputed to the believer. After that,

---

49. Thiessen, *Lectures in Systematic Theology*, 292–293.

begins the journey of sanctification in which we are in partnership with God in the act of discipleship both for ourselves and for others, to become like Jesus in our being and in our doing. While sanctification is the initiative of God, discipleship is the call of God to partner with Him in His act of sanctification, and IHD is a strategic ministry of discipleship for the work of sanctification.

Peter's inner healing after the resurrection

It is possible to interpret the events of John 21:15–17 from a DEW perspective to see how the "feet of Peter needed washing" after the resurrection of Christ. In John 21:15–17, after the resurrection of Christ, Jesus came to Peter to free him from the guilt and shame of his earlier denial of Jesus, when Jesus was arrested before His crucifixion. This baggage of guilt and shame was so important to Jesus that He specifically dealt with it so that the distance from Him, created by this emotional and mental baggage would be removed, and Peter would be free to pursue an intimate relationship with God, and to follow the destiny God had for him as His apostle. Peter would not have been able to enter into a greater intimate relationship with God nor enter into God's plan for him as a key apostle of the church, if Jesus had not brought an inner healing regarding his past.

This is what IHD does. It removes the baggage of the past through a process of helping the person let the Holy Spirit "put-off," release or empty out hurtful ungodly emotions (e.g. pain, anger, anxiety); ungodly thoughts or "strongholds" (which 2 Cor describes as ". . . every pretentious thought that sets itself against the knowledge of God"); and demonic spirits that may have had a foothold in our lives. We then help the person to align himself to God so that the Holy Spirit can "put-on," heal, fill up, or renew the mind with the emotions of the Kingdom (e.g., peace, joy, love, courage, hope, the fruit of the Spirit), and with the mind of God, to enable him to live a godly life.

This is sanctification, discipleship, and IHD taking place all at the same time, as God is doing the work of transformation through renewal and healing of the mind by the Holy Spirit. In the work of facilitating healing encounters, we are in fact "washing the feet of the believer." This healing gives the person the freedom to receive instruction, and creates the capacity for a healthy response to discipleship in the Word and for growth in God. Discipleship is enhanced as IHD is ministered to the believer, which

The Importance of IHD for Effective Discipleship

is part of the process of progressive sanctification in God. This is what Jesus did for Peter in this episode in John 21.

Peter had boasted that he would never deny Jesus even if it meant his death (Matt 26:33–35). Jesus said to Peter that before the cock crowed twice, Peter would deny Him three times (Matt 26:34). The night that Jesus was arrested, Peter denied Jesus three times when three different persons recognized him as being with Jesus, after which the cock crowed twice (Mark 14:66–72). Peter ran away, filled with the guilt and shame of his denial of Jesus, as it quickly came to his mind of what Jesus had said earlier, that whoever denies Jesus, the Father in heaven would likewise deny him.

On the day of the resurrection, Peter was at the tomb with the other disciples (John 20:1–2). They believed in who Jesus had said He was, when they found the tomb empty, except for the cloth that had wrapped the body of Jesus, including the face cloth. Jesus appeared to His disciples in a room they had gathered in, and they all believed (John 19–29), but they returned to being fishermen. While they were fishing (John 21:1–11), Jesus appeared to them again. They had not caught any fish until Jesus told them to throw the net on the right-hand side of the boat. When they did so, they caught so much fish that they were not able to haul in the catch. Peter was so astounded by the presence of Jesus that he jumped into the water. When Peter came to shore, Jesus had prepared a fire with some bread and fish. Jesus invited Peter and some of the disciples to eat breakfast. Peter knew and believed that Jesus was the Son of God, but the guilt and shame of his past denial (of Christ) kept him at a cautious distance from Jesus.

The distance between Peter and Jesus is made plain by the penetrating questions Jesus asked Peter. Jesus asked Peter if He *agape* Him, and Peter replied that he only *phileo* Him.[50] Peter had once declared that he would love the Lord even unto death but later on, had denied Jesus three times. Now gripped by guilt and shame, a distance separated Peter and Jesus. A baggage from the past consisting of pain and failure, convinced Peter that he could not fulfill the act of *agape* to the Lord. The past would pose a serious limitation to Peter's future growth in the Lord. If ever Peter was to grow in his relationship with Christ, this baggage of guilt and shame had to be expunged.

Seen from a DEW perspective, this event was a very significant healing moment for Peter. Jesus asked Peter twice if he could *agape* Him. Peter

---

50. *Agape* is a love that is fully committed while *phileo* speaks of a fond and affectionate love.

Linking Sanctification, IHD, and Discipleship

answered twice, with all honesty, that he could only *phileo* the Lord. Jesus accepted the answer of Peter and instructed Peter to feed his sheep. After the first two *agape* questions, Jesus asked Peter a third time, but this time, differently from the first two times. Jesus asked Peter whether Peter "phileo" Him (instead of *agape*). By this, Jesus revealed His total acceptance of where Peter was. This is why Peter said: "Lord, You know all things; You know that I only *phileo* You." It is as if Jesus was saying to Peter, "Peter, it is okay. I can accept this level of love from you. Let's begin from here—still, feed my sheep."

This is why Peter cried, because he saw how far he was from the Lord, and yet the Lord came so near to him to lift him up. Here was Peter in honesty, confessing remorsefully his deficient state of love for the Lord and then encountering firsthand, Jesus' offer of forgiveness, full acceptance, and restoration; a divine exchange had taken place that only Jesus could accomplish for Peter. Peter could not do it himself. Justification, regeneration and initial sanctification had already taken place at the empty tomb for Peter.

Now, Jesus was at work in progressive sanctification, bringing healing to Peter, who was trapped in guilt and shame, so that Peter would be released from the baggage of his past (specifically, the perception that his denial had consigned him as unworthy of the Lord, who loved him most). If Jesus had not done this for Peter, or if Peter had not allowed Jesus to do this for him, Peter would have been obstructed in his growth into the Lord's calling as a key apostle of the Gospel. It is all about being loved by Jesus and allowing Him to take the baggage of our past guilt and shame, healing us, and setting us free to grow in Him. This is Christ applying inner healing in God's process of sanctification. It redeems the person from past sins; frees them from the pain of rejection, shame, and guilt; sets him free from the bondage to past wrongs; removes the oppression of the enemy in his life; renews the mind, and releases him to grow in the Spirit without hindrances of the past; releases him to grow in his relationship with God, and to pursue the plans and purposes of God for his life, serving Him gratefully.

When inner healing is applied to discipleship, there is a healing redemptive transformation that is accomplished by Christ, and through the work of Christ, by the power of the Holy Spirit. Every believer has a past that needs to be healed so that they can enter into the fullness of their identity in Christ, and become wholly involved in the plans of God in reconciling the world to Himself. IHD is part of the work of discipleship in God's process of sanctification.

The Importance of IHD for Effective Discipleship

THE INTEGRAL CONNECTION OF DISCIPLESHIP, SANCTIFICATION, AND IHD

To understand the connection linking discipleship, sanctification and IHD, we have to first understand the work of the Holy Spirit. Jenney identifies the task of the Holy Spirit at this present stage of salvation history to include conviction of sin, cleansing the believer through the blood of Christ, impartation of Christ's righteousness to the believer, partnering the believer to disciple others in the process of sanctification, evangelizing and nurturing the growth of the believer.[51]

Jenney includes evangelizing the unbeliever as part of the work of sanctification. Whether you include this as part of the Holy Spirit's work of sanctification or not, discipleship encompasses a believer's response to all of the work of the Holy Spirit, both as a recipient and a discipler of others to make us (and them), more like Jesus.

James G. Samra defines discipleship as the continuous work of helping a person to grow into the likeness of Christ. He explains that discipleship starts at the point of salvation and continues on all through the life of the person, who works alongside with God in His work of sanctification. Samra says that true discipleship has two parts: teaching about Christ is the first part, followed by the imitation of those who are matured in Christ in their living and in their being.[52]

Samra elaborates that discipling is a process where the matured believer helps a younger believer on an individual basis or in a discipleship group. In both cases, it involves a genuine relationship that facilitates growth in soul-winning, humbleness, and the many aspects of the life of Christ that can be followed and evaluated. The process of discipling can be formal or informal, and may include disciplining or affirming a person.[53]

Samra suggests that all Christians are called to be actively involved in the discipleship process as a recipient of instructions, imitating the lives of those who follow Christ, and in turn being a discipler, who educates younger Christians and models Christ to them.[54] In other words, for discipleship to take place, it must be taught, received, and lived out. It is a transformation

---

51. Jenney, "Holy Spirit," 399.
52. Samra, "Biblical View," 234.
53. Samra, "Biblical View," 234.
54. Samra, "Biblical View," 234.

of a life from that lived at first without Christ, to one subsequently lived with Christ as Lord.

Stephen Bevans uses the term "transformed disciple," referring to a believer who makes a shift from being a mere passive uninvolved believer to a believer who actively lives out his life imitating and following Jesus as Christ and Lord.[55] This is radical discipleship—"thorough-going, committed, and deeply rooted; that is, it must become a way of life," and it involves sharing in the mission of Jesus.[56] In turn, sharing in the mission of Jesus includes evangelism, which Walter Brueggemann argues is an essential part of discipleship. He describes evangelism as "the invitation and summons to resituate our talk and our work according to the reality of this God," not just a church "recruitment of new members."[57] Samra also includes evangelism as part of discipleship, stating that discipleship begins with the entry into the discipleship process (salvation) and continues with growth (sanctification).[58]

From the discussion above concerning the idea of discipleship, it is clearly seen that discipleship concerns man's response to God's call to a relationship with Him, and God's work on the believer to become a new person matured in Christ in his being and doing, living for the purposes of God as Christ did. The disciple is one who lives his life according to his learning and understanding of how Jesus Christ lived His life—how Jesus lived His life becomes the disciple's praxis or way of life.[59] This description of a disciple reflects the meaning of the New Testament Greek word for disciples, *mathetes* (from the verb *mathanein*, "to learn"). It is about learning from the Christ in the gospels (Mark 1:7; Luke 4:27,33; Mark 10:39–40; Matt 10:24–25), and learning to live life by imitating how matured disciples of Christ in the Epistles lived their lives for God (2 Thess 3:7–9; Heb 13:7; 3 John 11; 1 Cor 4:16; 11:1; Eph 5:1; 1 Thess 1:6; 2:14; Heb 6:12; Phil 3:17; 1 Cor 7:7–11; Gal 4:12–20; Phil 4:9; Jas 5:10–11).[60] It is also noted that discipleship involves one as a disciple (a receiver learner), and also as a discipler (a teacher and model for others to follow or imitate).

---

55. Bevans, "Transforming Discipleship," 79.
56. Bevans, "Transforming Discipleship," 76–77.
57. Brueggemann, "Evangelism and Discipleship," 134.
58. Samra, "Biblical View," 234.
59. Bevans, "Transforming Discipleship," 76.
60. Samra, "Biblical View," 221–24.

The Importance of IHD for Effective Discipleship

In addition, the scope of discipleship is all encompassing of everything the Holy Spirit wants to do in and through a person's life—a person's "being" (who he is), and "doing" (how and for what purpose he lives life). It's about a willingness to totally embrace Jesus for who He is, and for what He has done, and for what He is doing today. Jeff Savage says that this is achieved by an absolute trust in Jesus, embracing the teachings and life of Jesus and teaching others about what Jesus taught and how He is being revealed in the bible.[61] He suggested that it is the practice of spiritual disciplines that enables the believer to embrace Jesus' teaching and lifestyle.[62] Spiritual disciplines is described as habitual activities that require the total involvement of our thinking, feeling and commitment of will to align our total personhood to become the very expression of His image, will and purposes.[63] Savage says the many practices of spiritual disciplines include: "worship, fellowship, prayer, fasting, study, service, solitude, sacrifice, secrecy, and confession." These are essential tools for our progression in spiritual maturity, and in engaging God in a relationship of intimacy that encounters and responds continuously to His grace.[64] It must be acknowledged that these have greatly helped many disciples in their spiritual growth, and in their development of an intimate relationship with God.

However, what can greatly help the effectiveness of the practice of spiritual disciplines is the healing of brokenness from the wounding of a person living in this fallen world. This healing gives freedom to the believer to participate more readily and responsively in these spiritual disciplines, opening the way for God to effectively transform the person for effective growth in Christlikeness and empowerment to fulfill the purposes of God. Gregory Nyssa recognized that the soul must first be cleansed and purified of sin before it can embrace divine perfection.[65] Sandra Wilson (at the beginning of this dissertation), and all the stories told, reflect the need to attend to these matters of the heart, experienced by all of us, albeit some to a greater extent than others.

IHD is not a spiritual discipline but an essential strategic ministry of discipleship, responding to the Holy Spirit's work of sanctification to cleanse the heart so that the disciple can truly embrace the work of God

---

61. Savage, "Toward 2000," 284.
62. Savage, "Toward 2000," 284–85.
63. Savage, "Toward 2000," 284.
64. Savage, "Toward 2000," 285.
65. Hill, "Rethinking Christian Identity," 122.

in forming Christ in their "being" and "doing." Discipleship involves the internal condition of the heart.[66] IHD should be considered as a ministry of discipleship that provides a focused avenue for the believer to encounter God, to "put-off" the old self and "put-on" the new self. This is a work of sanctification or transformation that is accomplished through intentional discipleship to form Christ in the disciple. The scope of discipleship is larger than IHD, because it encompasses responding to all that the Holy Spirit wants to do in and through the lives of believers. However, IHD is part of man's response to what the Holy Spirit wants to do, to cleanse the heart so that the believer is truly free to respond to the work of the Holy Spirit.

PRACTICAL THEOLOGY: CHRISTOPRAXIS

IHD—The participatio Christi factor in discipleship/practical theology

Unfortunately, over the course of church history, discipleship has concerned itself with living out a personal Christian ethic that is interpreted from the lifestyle of Christ—the *imitatio* of Christ which is merely the "imitation of Christ".[67] Few provisions were made in discipleship for an experience of *partipatio* or *participatio Christi* as in ontologically participating in the life of God through Christ.[68]

Modern Christianity has reduced sanctification to "the distinctive life-style of the committed soul."[69] Lifestyle is defined as the values and attitudes of a person and the accompanying behavior of a person.[70] What has become of sanctification is a progressive reduction of what is divine action on man, to that of human action to be like Christ, more like Christian ethics. The expressions of discipleship become more a living out of a personal Christian ethic that is interpreted from the lifestyle of Christ—the *imitatio* of Christ.[71] Andrew Root says that practical theology has refrained from acknowledging tangible evidences of the activities of God in the locales, deferring rather, to discuss extensively about human endeavors, activities

---

66. Shirley, "It Takes a Church," 211.
67. Root, *Christopraxis*, 81.
68. Root, *Christopraxis*, 73.
69. White, "Salvation,".
70. Moore and Elizabeth, "Transforming Church," 51–69.
71. Root, *Christopraxis*, 81.

and practices to live the Christian life.⁷² This has been the predominant direction of discipleship, the main expression of practical theology. Discipleship has for a long time been just an imitation of Christ in the realm of the ethics of living life as Christ did. Meanwhile, the work of Christ (e.g. signs, wonders, healings, and deliverance), has often been relegated to the background, while Christian ethics, including man's efforts to imitate Christ, have been brought to the foreground, taking the form of spiritual disciplines.

The inclusion of IHD in discipleship adds the *participatio Christi* factor, so that discipleship becomes more than just *imitatio Christi* but includes an encounter and participation with God that transforms lives. A theological construct that helps with the acceptance, understanding, and explaining of divine actions in human experience such as signs and wonders and IHD, is called Christopraxis. This construct has been adopted in Practical Theology by some theologians like Andrew Roots and Ray S. Anderson.

Christopraxis—A theological construct that supports IHD in discipleship

Practical Theology as a discipline seeks to connect the current church praxis with God's current continued mission in fulfilling His purposes for and in the world we live in, to establish the integrity of the church praxis in serving God's purposes.⁷³ Praxis is more than just practice because praxis is an active energized practice that is motivated by and committed to a theory.⁷⁴ In this case, the church praxis must serve the theory of God's missional purpose and the reality of His activity in our world, for the good of humanity.⁷⁵ Ray writes that the science of interpretation in practical theology attempts to explain what is naturally in Jesus Christ, the very authority of God, and the tangible recognizable demonstration of Christ's presence in the acts of the Holy Spirit in the practice of ministry.⁷⁶ The ministry praxis of the church must, therefore, be the expression of the ministry of the risen Christ through the Holy Spirit (who manifests the ministry of the risen and ascended Christ), congruent with Scriptures and today's experiential

---

72. Root, *Christopraxis*, 13.
73. Anderson, *Shape of Practical Theology*, 22.
74. Anderson, *Shape of Practical Theology*, 47.
75. Anderson, *Shape of Practical Theology*, 24–25.
76. Anderson, *Shape of Practical Theology*, 38.

realities of divine action.⁷⁷ The continued ministry, person and presence of Christ is "seen", experienced and encountered in the ministry of the church through the works of the Holy Spirit.⁷⁸ This is the fundamental premise of the Christopraxis theological construct of Practical Theology.

Root says that the Christopraxis construct is not just an interpretive function of what God is doing through the church, but an actual ontological joining of God and man in ministry. As Root puts it, it is "the unveiling of God's self (becoming)—it is the event of an ontological encounter."⁷⁹ Roots describes it as ontological because it can be seen that God is present Himself to minister to humankind, and He gives His ministry fully through our ontological being in full expressions of His presence, so real that the presence of Christ is seen revealing God to man, and reconciling man back to God.⁸⁰ Root further explains that God gives Himself to us by manifesting His presence through us in our work of touching lives. This is seen as God partnering with us in real action terms, not just imitations. He says that in choosing to be in partnership with God in ministry, we are involved ontologically with Him, and not just behaviorally. God's presence is actually with us in the operation of ministry, and He participates with us and through us, in ministry.⁸¹

This means that we engage God ontologically in the action of ministry, ontologically manifesting the presence of Christ in action in His power, His authority, His work, His truth, and His love, in which is found the abundance of His grace. All of this happens for us via the presence of the Holy Spirit, who is the presence of Christ, in us. The call of Jesus to wash each other's feet is one such initiative of God to be ontologically involved with Christ in His work of sanctification. Initial positional sanctification is imputed to us through the completed work of Christ in His death and resurrection for us, when we are justified through our faith in Christ. We are called to participate actively in progressive sanctification into being like Christ through discipleship that involves being taught and teaching others to follow Jesus. This is the real objective and call of Jesus to His disciples to wash each other's feet—involvement in progressive sanctification. Peter had refused Jesus to wash his feet and Jesus replied: "If I do not wash you,

77. Anderson, *Shape of Practical Theology*, 38.
78. Anderson, *Shape of Practical Theology*, 54.
79. Root, *Christopraxis*, 94.
80. Root, *Christopraxis*, 95.
81. Root, *Christopraxis*, 96.

The Importance of IHD for Effective Discipleship

you have no part with Me." (John 13:8) The act of washing the disciples' feet was all about being a part of who Christ is. Peter's reply is for the Lord to wash all of him. To which Jesus replies: "He who has bathed needs only to wash his feet, but is completely clean; and you are clean" (John 13:10). The disciple having had a bath and is clean, is likened to God's initial positional sanctification of us, but it follows that we must continually be formed by Him, to come into the fullness of our positional sanctification, by allowing our feet to be washed by Christ.

Jesus then says to his disciples that they must continuously do what He had just done for them, so that they will be blessed. This whole act of foot washing was done at a point in time when it would be His last supper with them. He would thereafter be crucified and resurrected by God the Father, and would ascend to heaven. After that, the Holy Spirit would come upon the disciples and they would then be ontologically joined with God in the action of ministry. Christ would then continue to be present ontologically in and through the ministry of His disciples, as they washed each other's feet, to help each other become more and more like Christ. The act of discipleship is the act of following Christ in being discipled (having their feet washed by others), and discipling others (the act of washing someone else's feet)—all of which mirror Christ's call for us to be involved ontologically in God's work of progressive sanctification.

God's work of progressive sanctification must involve the restoration of the wholeness of man, just as Christ restored Peter, so that Peter could fully enter into his involvement in Christ's assignment to feed His sheep. This is what IHD does. It is the involvement of a disciple of Jesus Christ together with Christ by the Holy Spirit, to "wash the feet" of another disciple. This is an ontological involvement in the ministry of Christ to bring wholeness to a disciple of Jesus Christ, resolving the past guilt, shame, hurts and other bondages of the past. The disciple is then truly released into his journey of entering into personhood with Christ "to be" and "to do" as Christ did, in living His life for the glory of God. It is about replicating the charismatic ministry of Jesus Christ in the discipleship of believers.

Jon Ruthven says that these days, the study of Christ has a strong spiritual context that acknowledges that a key idea of the New Testament in the charismatic ministry of Jesus is that His ministry is meant to be reproduced by others in the same expressions of His power and presence.[82] Ruthven maintains that Jesus made it known clearly that His disciples are to replicate

---

82. Ruthven, "Imitation of Christ," 60–78.

His work exactly, and in every generation of mankind.[83] His argument is that the cultural and religious background of the teacher and student relationship during the time of Jesus was one that bound the teaching and practice of the life of the teacher to the student to such an extent, that every disciple replicates the lessons, the being and doings of the discipler.[84] Ruthven cites Christ's rigidity of the disciples replicating his ministry in the pattern of "As I . . . so you," in Luke 6:40; John 13:34; 17:18, 23; and 20:21. He also points at Jesus' usage of the word "as" (*kathos*) in John 13:15 and John 20:21, which he takes to mean "very close, identical, and not just a similarity without being the same."[85] In John 13:15, Jesus said: "For I gave you an example that you also should do as (*kathos*) I did to you." Ruthven explains that in the time of Jesus, it was the tradition of the Palestinian Jews for disciples to replicate as exactly as possible every known fact of a teacher's life.[86] Paul said the same in 1 Cor 11:1 when he said: "Be imitators of me, just as (*kathos*) I also am of Christ"—meaning "to the same degree and extent that I imitate Christ".[87] He repeated this instruction to imitate Him four other times to the churches (1 Cor 4:16; Phil 3:17; 2 Thess 3:7, 9; cf. Gal 4:12, Phil 4:9; Jas 3:1; 1 Tim 4:16; 2 Tim 3:4).[88]

The purpose of the ministry of Jesus is described as "to destroy the works of the Devil," in 1 John 3:8. Peter's description of the ministry of Christ in Acts 10:38 is: "God anointed Jesus of Nazareth with the Holy Spirit and with power . . . He went around doing good and there were numerous reports of Jesus' acts of healings and exorcism." Ruthven points out the percentages of miracles recorded as: 44 percent of Matthew, 65 percent of Mark, 29 percent of Luke, 30 percent of John, and 27 percent of Acts.[89] Jesus also sent the disciples to replicate His ministry in Mark 3:14–15 in preaching and casting out demons. The Great Commission in Mark 16:15–18 is Jesus' instruction to continue His ministry in the miraculous—"These signs will accompany those who believe: in My name they will cast out demons, they will speak in new tongues . . ."

83. Ruthven, "Imitation of Christ," 66.
84. Ruthven, "Imitation of Christ," 66.
85. Ruthven, "Imitation of Christ," 69.
86. Ruthven, "Imitation of Christ," 69.
87. Ruthven, "Imitation of Christ," 70.
88. Ruthven, "Imitation of Christ," 70.
89. Ruthven, "Imitation of Christ," 72–73.

The Importance of IHD for Effective Discipleship

God is not just transcendent as some have suggested, but He is also immanent. He is ontologically present in the disciples of Jesus Christ by His Holy Spirit, Who is also the Spirit of Christ. Hence Christ is also present in and through the Holy Spirit's presence in our lives. Our relationship with Jesus Christ is ontological, as much as is the case, with our ministry to one another via the Holy Spirit. In the work of sanctification, God has imputed an initial positional status of sanctification, a righteousness, and holiness of Christ, to us whilst He works at us entering into the fullness of the positional status of sanctification bringing into reality the person of Christ in us, in who we are, and in what we do. This is the process of sanctification that He invites us to participate with Him, through our involvement in discipleship. In the process of discipleship, the ministry of IHD can truly bring our past under the blood of Jesus for healing, restoration, and liberation from the baggage of our past (which has hurts, sins, and spiritual strongholds of the enemy). This allows us to be truly free to align ourselves to all of who Christ is in His being and doing, intimately knowing God the Father.

4

Where Might God be Placing the IHD Ministry?

IN THIS CHAPTER OF church history, we look at how the church, over the years, has accepted and committed itself to the ministry of Jesus, in His acts of healing and deliverance, including the working of miracles, signs, and wonders. The exploration and investigation will utilize the timeline of church history: Old Testament, New Testament, Apostolic Church Period, Medieval Church History, Reformation Period, and the present Twentieth Century Era. The desired aim is a better understanding of how the church has gotten to where it is, with regards to her acceptance of, and commitment to, the IHD ministry. The historical analysis would also help us better discern how we should be developing this ministry further, and how God could be guiding the IHD ministry into its next important steps.

EXPLORING THE OLD TESTAMENT

A brief look at the Old Testament's records on human suffering presents a good starting point for establishing Christian beliefs on evil, sickness, demons, and God. The ministry of inner healing and deliverance today harkens back to the healing ministry of Jesus that includes deliverance of a person from demonic spirits and the restoration of a sound mind.

The Importance of IHD for Effective Discipleship

Wonsuk Ma wrote that ancient Isrealites had an understanding of the source of evil in the context of Satan and demonic spirit[1]. According to him, this worldview of the Israelites was constructed by two groups of people. First, the prophets, priests and scribes who set the foundation for all religious and social beliefs and lifestyle. Second, the traditional legends, beliefs, religious and spiritual practices of Israel's neighboring communities.[2] Ma notes that the ancient Israelites believed that there were evil forces of a supernatural sort actually in operation. They did not fully understand these evil forces, although they did have usage of terms such as demons, spirits and princes. Indeed, these terms were often incorporated into their spiritual practices of a demonic nature, as seen in Balaam's planned curse.[3] Satan was also exposed as an agent of evil, who was an accuser in the story of Job (Job 1:6-11), bringing disaster and raging havoc (Job 1:16; 19; 2:7).[4] The worldview of God, Satan and the spirit realm was never a myth to them, but reality. Folkloric representations such as deep sea dragons and other forces, subdued by God, were pervasive from early on.[5]

Ma notes that there exists only a few references to spirits of a malevolent nature, as (in) a distinctive entity, in the Old Testament. These include demonic spirits in the episode of Abimelech and the people residing in Sechem (Judg 9:23); the tormenting of Saul by a demonic spirit (1 Sam 16:15; 16:23; 18:10; 19:9); and the spirit of lies that dominated Ahab's prophets (1 Kgs 22:22, 23;2 Chr 18:21, 22).[6] Ma opines that that there are other spirit references that are mentioned, but not necessarily with reference to an individual spirit being, and these include a "spirit of judgment" and a "spirit of fire" (Isa 4:4), a "spirit of dizziness" (Isa 19:14) and a "spirit of prostitution" (Hos 4:12, 5:4).[7]

The case of King Saul in the Old Testament is the only clear reference to demonic spirits causing a mental and emotional disturbance (1 Sam 16:16, 23).[8] The evil spirit had both internal and external effects. Ma explains that Saul was greatly disturbed internally by an evil spirit that

---

1. Kay and Parry, *Exorcism & Deliverance*, 27.
2. Kay and Parry, *Exorcism & Deliverance*, 27–28.
3. Kay and Parry, *Exorcism & Deliverance*, 43.
4. Kay and Parry, *Exorcism & Deliverance*, 40.
5. Kay and Parry, *Exorcism & Deliverance*, 28.
6. Kay and Parry, *Exorcism & Deliverance*, 32.
7. Kay and Parry, *Exorcism & Deliverance*, 32.
8. Kay and Parry, *Exorcism & Deliverance*, 33.

Where Might God be Placing the IHD Ministry?

made him desperate for a relief (1 Sam 16:15; 16:23). The knowledge that a person's mental torment and headaches can be the result of activities of demonic spirits was well known over the many cultures in the region of ancient East.[9] The external effect reared its head in the evil spirit urging Saul to kill David.[10]

Ma points out three important things about evil spirits. First, they are the cause of mental torment and are instigators of harm and wickedness. Second, people who were near to Saul recognized the evidence of the presence of evil spirits (16:15).[11] Third, evil spirits could be eliminated by human effort. I would not fully agree with the third point though. Ma is of the opinion that the torments and disturbances of evil spirits can be reduced, alleviated and even eliminated by the works of man. He cites the instance in which Saul's courtier recommended that a skillful harp player be called upon to provide relief to Saul. David's music on the harp and songs did its intended job, bringing relief to Saul, with the spirits actually leaving Saul, on one occasion (1 Sam 16:16, 23).[12]

The use of King David as a point of evidence that evil spirits can be eliminated by human effort, fails to consider that David had an anointing from God. The servant of Saul who introduced David said in 1 Sam 16:18, "Behold I have seen a son of Jesse the Bethlehemite who is a skillful musician, a mighty man of valor, a warrior, one prudent in speech and a handsome man, and the Lord is with him." King Saul's servant recommended David to King Saul, only after David had been anointed as a chosen servant of God to be king by Samuel in 1 Sam 16:12 -13. David himself acknowledged in 1 Sam 17:37, that it was the Lord who gave him the strength to defeat a lion and a bear, in his youth. Hence it is still the anointing of the Lord working through David's music that soothed King Saul and caused the departure of the evil spirits. The evidence is that God was working through David.

Ma says that the worldview of the ancient Israelites depicts the existence of good and evil as being submitted to the sovereignty of God as seen in the Creation story, where at the beginning of creation, God created both light and darkness, and there was no evidence that there ever was any struggle of darkness with God. He claims that the most important truth

---

9. Kay and Parry, *Exorcism & Deliverance*, 33.
10. Kay and Parry, *Exorcism & Deliverance*, 33.
11. Kay and Parry, *Exorcism & Deliverance*, 34.
12. Kay and Parry, *Exorcism & Deliverance*, 34.

established in the Old Testament is the absolute supremacy of Yahweh, Who is the "all loving and all powerful God who holds the key to all the problems of evil."[13] According to Ma, no other spirits are given acknowledgement as "full blown deities."[14] This truth is reflected clearly in the ministry of Jesus in His practice of healing and deliverance.

While the knowledge of evil forces and demonic spirits is acknowledged in Old Testament literature, there is little known record of divine healing, exorcism, and deliverance. Ma notes that the mention of the eviction of demonic spirits increased significantly only after the Old Testament period. The Qumran document is an example of written references of a theology that included demonic spirits and Satan that increasingly developed during the inter-testamental period.[15] The New Testament, beginning with Jesus, began a new era of the display of the reality of the spirit realm, its focus on evil spirits destroying man, but superseded by the work of God through Christ, bringing healing to man from sinister causes of man's suffering.

THE HEALING AND DELIVERANCE MINISTRY OF CHRIST IN THE NEW TESTAMENT

Andrew Daunton-Fear offers a comprehensive summary of the New Testament record of Jesus' ministry of healing and deliverance. He concluded that a major theme of the four gospels in the New Testament is the impressive healing ministry of Jesus Christ. He recounts twenty-two stories (excluding parallel accounts) of the powerful works of healing that Jesus did. These include the accounts of the three persons that He raised from the dead, four incidences of evicting demonic spirits, and fifteen cases of different physical healings—three cases of blindness, two body paralysis, two leprosy cases, fever, recovering a shriveled hand, a case of excessive bleeding, a hearing recovery, a bent back, dropsy, reattachment of an ear that was cut off, and a terminal death case. In addition there were many passing references of healing and exorcism.[16]

Different authors and scholars have accounted for the number and variety of healings differently, depending on what is being considered.

13. Kay and Parry, *Exorcism & Deliverance*, 44.
14. Kay and Parry, *Exorcism & Deliverance*, 44.
15. Kay and Parry, *Exorcism & Deliverance*, 43.
16. Daunton-Fear, *Healing*, 1.

Morton Kelsey has a list of thirty reported healings in the New Testament.[17] However, all agree that there are indeed many recorded incidents of healing and deliverance or exorcism, some to individuals, some to multitudes. Most scholars and authors look at deliverance or exorcism as clearly a part of the healing ministry of Jesus.

The question that arises then is: "What is the intent of the ministry of healing and deliverance or exorcism?" There are several suggestions. A popular suggestion is that Jesus intended it as "proofs" of His divinity.[18] Percy Dearmer argues that these are acts of kindness reflecting the compassion of Christ, and not mere proofs of His divinity.[19] Alfred Plummer says that while the acts of healing are primarily acts of beneficence, they are secondarily used to establish His credential of authority.[20] James Dunn suggests that Christ's healing and miracles ministry "was evidence that the longed-for kingdom of God had already come upon His hearers."[21]

Robert Dickinson gives another suggestion that the healing miracles of Christ are proofs of the "power and authority of Christ, as presented by Himself."[22] Kelsey asserts that the healing miracles of Jesus were a sign and a basic credential and evidence that the Kingdom of Heaven was breaking forth into this world, and that He (Jesus) was the Messiah.[23] Dickinson based his assertion on the answer that Jesus gave to the disciples of John, who came to inquire as to who He was, in Matt 11:4–5. Jesus replied: "Go back and report to John what you hear and see; the blind receive sight, and the lame walk, the lepers are cleansed, and the deaf hear, and the dead are raised and the good news is proclaimed to the poor."[24]

While all the above discussions are important, Amanda Porterfield suggested that though the healing and exorcism miracles of Jesus are fundamental to the meaning of discipleship, this relationship between the works of healing and discipleship has not been properly acknowledged. Two reasons are cited by her for this obscurity—disagreements on Jesus'

17. Kelsey, *Healing and Christianity*. 44.
18. Dickinson, *God Does Heal Today*, 16.
19. Dickinson, *God Does Heal Today*, 16.
20. Dickinson, *God Does Heal Today*, 17.
21. Kydd, *Healing Through the Centuries*, 10.
22. Dickinson, *God Does Heal Today*, 19.
23. Kelsey, *Healing and Christianity*, 46.
24. Kelsey, *Healing and Christianity*, 46.

The Importance of IHD for Effective Discipleship

intention with regards to healing, and the continuous varying interpretations by many through the years.[25]

If what she says is true, the question then is: "Has the church missed altogether, the importance and significance of healing and deliverance in the process of discipleship that was demonstrated, and perhaps then, meant to be a part of the restoration and transformation of man into the image of Christ?"

The transformation value relating to discipleship seen in Jesus' act of exorcism and deliverance was noted by John Woolmer. For instance, Jesus told the man He freed at the pool of Bethesda to stop sinning lest recurrence of the sickness will be worse than what he had previously suffered.[26] He told the woman in adultery to leave her life of sin (John 8:11). Those freed from evil spirits were warned of a final state that would be worse, if they continued in sin (Matt 12:45).[27] Woolmer pointed out that Jesus actually meant "wholeness", as in being made well (e.g., Luke 8:48), in the use of the Greek verb (*sozo*), instead of the often translated meaning, saved (e.g. Luke 7:50). Jesus was looking at transforming the lives of every person in the many episodes of healing, teaching, and even in the many other non-healing encounters.[28] Hence, Jesus was doing discipleship when He did healings for people, just as much as in all of His other ministry of intervening in people's lives, to help them.[29] He also pointed out that a clear evidence of Jesus' concern for the wholeness of the person (as is clear in His work of transformational healing and restoration), is seen in two different events—the Samaritan leper (Luke 17:11), and the woman with a sinful reputation that anointed Him (Luke 7:50). The point is being made here that it was not just physical wellness, but wholeness as a person, the restoration and transformational healing of the total person that matters to God.[30] Is this not the mark of Christian discipleship and should not exorcism/deliverance and inner healing then be part of the integrated process of discipleship?

It is also necessary for us to consider John Meier's observation that Jesus was a person playing many different roles with equal importance. He

25. Porterfield, *Healing in the History*, 41.
26. Woolmer, *Healing and Deliverance*, 86.
27. Woolmer, *Healing and Deliverance*, 86.
28. Woolmer, *Healing and Deliverance*, 85.
29. Woolmer, *Healing and Deliverance*, 85.
30. Woolmer, *Healing and Deliverance*, 85.

cast out demons, did miracle healings, taught morals, discipled many, and He was additionally an evangelist and an end-time prophet. Jesus was all of that in one person.[31] The importance of this observation is that Jesus always took an integrated approach, and saw the person as an integrated whole. In other words, the ministry of Jesus is comprehensive and transformative at the same time. It is His teaching, His relationship with His disciples, His ministry of exorcism and healing, and His activity as a prophet, that combine to produce effective discipleship. Kelsey holds a similar view and affirms that Jesus uses many different methods of ministry—teaching, acts of love and kindness—as expressions of God's mercy, with a definite flow of the power of God to heal, restore and touch lives, drawing people to God. Having drawn the people to a relationship with God, He began to teach them.[32] Broadhead affirms that Jesus' act of casting out demons, miracle healings and work of restoring people to wholeness, gave Him a strong theological basis, and the right to claim Messiahship and a rendering to His meaning of discipleship.[33]

This being the case, the act of exorcism is an important initial thrust that releases a person into a discipleship momentum and of transformation in the discipleship process.

John Carroll says that people encounter the heart of God to bring wholeness to man in both the teachings and acts of healings of Jesus.[34] He states that God's intent in bringing wholeness through the works of healing, casting out demons, and miracles was to bring a transformative change of the heart (*metanoia*) towards a wholehearted commitment to submit to the rule of God.[35]

Meier argues that Jesus clearly implied this when he addressed Chorazin and Bethsaida (Matt11:20-24; Luke 10:13-15). "Woe to you, Chorazin! Woe to you, Bethsaida! For if the miracles had occurred in Tyre and Sidon which occurred in you, they would have repented (*metanoesan*) long ago (sitting) in sackcloth and ashes." Meier says that the acts of miracles, and of healing and deliverance from demons, are not stand alone acts of God's goodness, but are an integrated part of God's call to a commitment to trusting and obeying His will. This is the intended result of all the acts of God in

---

31. Porterfield, *Healing in the History*, 37.
32. Kelsey, *Healing and Christianity*, 69.
33. Porterfield, *Healing in the History*, 37.
34. Carroll, "Sickness & Healing," 130.
35. Carroll, "Sickness & Healing," 137.

The Importance of IHD for Effective Discipleship

healing.[36] In other words, healing is a good start for the process of transformation, but there must be a commitment to live life according to the will of God after healing has taken place. The process of discipleship should reinforce resoluteness to live a transformed life in, and for the Lord.

Carroll makes the important observation that today's interpreters have run into great difficulties in accepting the language of demonic possession and exorcism, preferring instead, the language of science and psychology, and are quick to relegate the former to mythology based on an outmoded worldview. Regardless of how one chooses to interpret the miracles of healing, Meier says that many of Jesus' acts of healing are in fact exorcism. This indicates that the problems of man are not just in the issue of sin, but also in the liberation from oppression, and the confronting of the kingdom of Satan.[37]

The seventy disciples, on their mission to preach the good news, healed the sick and cast out demons. It says in Luke 10:17—"Lord even the demons are subject to us in Your name"; and Jesus replied in Luke 10:18—"I saw Satan fall like lightning from heaven."[38] These verses underscore the high relevance of the ministry of healing, which confronts the kingdom of Satan, in addition to healing the emotional and psychological disorders of man. IHD sets people free to grow under discipleship.

Graham Twelftree made several observations underlining what seems like the varying importance of exorcism in the four gospels, which He says reflects, tellingly, the varying degrees of commitment and involvement of the Christian community in exorcism. He surmises that in the gospel of Mark, exorcism was highly profiled, whilst in Luke a more balanced depiction of the teaching ministry and the healing activities is noted, without over-emphasizing the ministry of deliverance.[39] Twelftree opines that Matthew probably gave low priority to miracles because Matthew was placing it behind the importance of the spoken word.[40] As for the Johannine literature, Twelftree says that the emphasis was on the teaching of salvation—what it means to have a relationship with Jesus. Although demon-related issues are present, they were not talked about much.[41] Twelftree notes that

---

36. Carroll, "Sickness & Healing," 137.
37. Carroll, "Sickness & Healing," 142.
38. Maddocks, *Christian Healing Ministry*, 55.
39. Kay and Perry, *Exorcism and Deliverance*, 68.
40. Kay and Perry, *Exorcism and Deliverance*, 63.
41. Kay and Perry, *Exorcism and Deliverance*, 68.

Where Might God be Placing the IHD Ministry?

the community of Mark's gospel, the earliest gospel to be written in Rome around 70 AD, was most involved in exorcism and healing demonstrated by the centrality of miracles, healing, and exorcism/deliverance.[42] He argues that Luke, Matthew, and John's lack of a similar emphasis is indicative that their communities were not as involved in healing and exorcism as Mark's was.[43] As for whether this is the right conclusion, is cause for moot.

It is important also to consider the call and the mission that Jesus entrusted to His disciples. In Luke 10:1,8,9 Jesus called the twelve disciples together and gave them power and authority to drive out all demons and cure diseases, and He sent them out to preach the Kingdom of God and to heal the sick (Luke 9:1,2). He sent them out in twos to many towns and said to them: "When you enter a town and are welcomed, eat what is set before you. Heal the sick who are there and tell them, 'The Kingdom of God is near you.'"

Francis MacNutt states that Jesus gave His disciples authority to preach His message of salvation with power accompanying it, to set the people free from their sinful state.[44] J.M. Creed argues that this event of Jesus sending out his disciples is not a general commissioning event nor a call to a general practice, but a directive for a specific dispensation of God's power given to both the Jews and the Gentiles as demonstrated by the ministry of the twelve disciples and the seventy Gentile disciples.[45] However which way one interprets this event, the fact remains that power and authority was given to the disciples to bring healing and deliverance from demonic spirits.

The book of Mark (Mark 16: 17) has the only record of the commissioning of Jesus to the Twelve, the Seventy, and all "those who believe", to heal the sick.[46] In the other accounts of Jesus' final commission to the disciples (Mat.28:19, 20; Acts 1:8), there is no clear instruction to bring healing, but only to preach and to teach.[47] J. Wilkinson has the same conclusion on the original gospel tradition.[48] Wilkinson then suggests that this is probably a later addition to the gospel of Mark and that the intent of the addition was

---

42. Kay and Perry, *Exorcism and Deliverance*, 58.
43. Kay and Perry, *Exorcism and Deliverance*, 68.
44. MacNutt, *Healing*, 57.
45. Dickinson, *God Does Heal Today*, 28.
46. Dickinson, *God Does Heal Today*, 31.
47. Dickinson, *God Does Heal Today*, 31.
48. Wilkinson, *Health and Healing*, 84.

The Importance of IHD for Effective Discipleship

to accept the probability that Jesus might have made the instruction, hence making allowance for the church to have Christ's authority to exercise His ministry of healing.[49] In addition, Wilkinson's final conclusion is that it is most likely the case that Jesus did not give explicit terms of healing to His disciples, but only of preaching and of being a witness.[50]

Most scholars agree with Dickinson that there is little record of healing and deliverance on the part of the original twelve disciples and Apostles, in the early days of the church.[51] According to Dickinson, there were significantly less recorded incidences of healing miracles in the book of Acts than during the time of the ministry of Jesus.[52] Morris Maddock points out that healing took place as long as the disciples acted in obedience to what Jesus taught them.[53] Dickinson also points out that there is neither any record of the fulfillment of a healing commission nor "any general program of healing."[54] MacNutt points out that although most of the recorded miracles in Acts and the epistles recorded mostly the acts of healing and deliverance by Paul and Peter (examples are found in Acts 3:1; 5:12; 5:16; 9:32; 9:36; 14:8; 19:11; 20:7; 28:7; 28:9), it is reasonable to accept that healing also happened through the ministry of all of the disciples. Some references made of Philip, Stephen and Ananias of Damascus support this suggestion.[55]

Only one case of deliverance from evil can be found in the Acts of the Apostles (16:16-18)—the case of the demon-possessed girl who harassed Paul continuously, following after him wherever he went.[56] MacNutt says evidence of healing is also indicated in Acts 4:29, 30 as the persecuted disciples and apostles prayed for the Lord to intervene in the threats experienced, to enable them to preach with great courage, and for the Lord to perform miracles.[57] MacNutt asserts that "the same Spirit Who empowered Jesus in His life and work is meant to empower the mission of the church."[58]

---

49. Wilkinson, *Health and Healing*, 84.
50. Wilkinson, *Health and Healing*, 84.
51. Dickinson, *God Does Heal Today*, 27.
52. Dickinson, *God Does Heal Today*, 31.
53. Maddocks, *Christian Healing Ministry*, 85.
54. Dickinson, *God Does Heal Today*, 31.
55. MacNutt, *Healing*, 59.
56. Dickinson, *God Does Heal Today*, 32.
57. MacNutt, *Healing*, 58.
58. MacNutt, *Healing*, 58.

There are three other evidences of healing and deliverance in the early church during the times of the disciples. James 2:19 implies that the apostles dealt with the demoniacs. It says, "You believe that God is one; you do well. Even the demons believe—and shudder (*phrissein*)."[59] The other evidence is found in 1 Cor 12:9-10, 28-30. Twelftree suggests that it can be extrapolated from this verse that exorcism was considered as a gift to be exercised.[60] Twelftree pointed at Heb 2:3-4 that says, "God also testifying with them, both by signs and wonders and various miracles (*dunamesin*) and by gifts (*merismois*) of the Holy Spirit according to His own will." Twelftree believes that the phase 'signs and wonders and various miracles' included exorcism, and is evidence that exorcism continued to accompany the preaching of the salvation message and was the showcase of the presence of God in and with the believer.[61] There is sufficient evidence to suggest that exorcism and healing were active expressions of the life of Christian ministry.

THE EARLY CHURCH

Healing and deliverance as a practice was part of Jesus' ministry and of the early church, especially the first 200 years following the New Testament recorded apostolic period.[62] To Porterfield, exorcism was an act of discipleship that dramatically displayed Christ's power to expel sin and evil from others and to heal them in the name of Jesus, and also a means of Christian outreach.[63] She writes that a hallmark of early Christianity was the ministry of exorcism, and that it was the reputation of those called Christians, who identified themselves as having God's power to confront evil.[64] According to Porterfield, the early church historian S.V. MacCasland identified exorcism as the most outstanding mark of discipleship far above teaching and preaching in the early church.[65] In addition, Porterfield notes that Ramsey MacMullen, a reputable Roman historian, also acknowledged that exorcism was an important ministry of Christians in second and third

---

59. Kay and Parry, *Exorcism & Deliverance*, 67.
60. Kay and Parry, *Exorcism & Deliverance*," 67.
61. Kay and Parry, *Exorcism & Deliverance*, 66–67.
62. Kelsey, *Healing and Christianity*, 104.
63. Porterfield, *Healing in the History*, 63.
64. Porterfield, *Healing in the History*, 63.
65. Porterfield, *Healing in the History*, 63.

The Importance of IHD for Effective Discipleship

century Christianity. He described it as a battle with 'nasty-lower powers' that dominates the victims' lives and which caused many kinds of oppressions and sufferings.[66]

Early writings of theologians such as Tertullian, Origen, and Irenaeus acknowledged the practice of healing. Eusebius, the bishop of Ceaserea in the early fourth century, who was also known as the 'Father of Church History,' recorded that the Gospel spread to many places as many went all over the world to preach the message of salvation.[67] Many functioned as evangelists, with God's grace and power accompanying their message demonstrating the presence of God. As a result many became Christians because they saw the power of God at work at the preaching of the Gospel.[68]

Origen (185–232 AD), a third-century theologian in the Eastern Church, in his treatise, *Against Celsus*, writes openly of healings and deliverance among the early church: "They expelled evil spirits, performed many cures, and foresaw certain events, according to the will of the Logos."[69] In defending the name of Christ, Origen adds: "And the name of Jesus can still remove distractions from the minds of men, and expel demons, and also take away diseases."[70] Origen noted that even uneducated Christians, who were illiterate, performed the work of evicting demons by mere prayers and commands.[71]

Cyprian (249 AD), the bishop of Carthage, in the third century wrote that the healing power of Christ was evident in the sacraments, especially in the sacrament of baptism for believers, during which many experienced deliverance.[72] He wrote that many who were baptized with conditions of terminal illness received the grace of God, were delivered from unclean spirits, and continued to live lives praising and honoring God as they continued to mature in faith.[73] He added that the demons who left spoke of yielding to the name and authority of the true God to leave the bodies of those they had inhabited.[74]

66. Porterfield, *Healing in the History*, 63.
67. Sawvelle, *Case For Healing*, 78.
68. Sawvelle, *Case For Healing*, 78.
69. Sawvelle, *Case For Healing*, 78.
70. Sawvelle, *Case For Healing*, 78.
71. Sawvelle, *Case For Healing*, 78
72. Sawvelle, *Case For Healing*, 79.
73. Sawvelle, *Case For Healing*, 79.
74. MacMullen, *Christianizing*, 27.

Where Might God be Placing the IHD Ministry?

Tertullian (240 AD), the Father of Latin Christianity, declared that Christians had authority over demons.[75] He wrote to the proconsul of North Africa of several cases of healing and deliverance. One such case involved a clerk who was set free from a spirit that constantly threw him to the ground. Tertullian also testified of many from different social statuses, from the commoners to the educated, who were set free of demonic spirits and healed of diseases.[76] MacNutt asserts that Tertullian claimed that the most noble thing Christians can do is to do the work of deliverance from evil spirits and to perform miracle healings, as they live their lives for God.[77]

Sawvelle writes that many heathens in the Roman Empire became Christians as they experienced and witnessed how the early believers brought healing to the sick and deliverance from demonic spirits.[78] He makes reference to Irenaeus' (202 AD) treatise *Against Heresis* that the true disciples of Jesus received grace from God to perform miracles, and that they drove demons from many who quickly believed in Christ and became Christians. Iranaeus noted that the same conversion happened for many who were healed by Christians laying hands on the sick and they experienced being restored to wholeness.[79]

MacNutt observes that the early church, right up to the fourth century, expected all who were baptized to receive the baptism in the Holy Spirit at the time of their water baptism.[80] Preparation for water baptism took up to two or three years, and part of that preparation included extensive teaching alongside the occurrence of exorcism. This was viewed as necessary because the early church understood from their ministry practice that the heathen converts were convinced of the truth of the gospel, as they knew full well the reality of the demonics, which had always been a part of the heathen culture.[81] Exorcism was also done on infants who received baptism as a precaution based on the belief that infants might have picked up demonic spirits from the demonic environment of their parents.[82]

---

75. Sawvelle, *Case for Healing*, 79.
76. Sawvelle, *Case For Healing*, 80.
77. MacNutt, *Healing Reawakening*, 83.
78. Sawvelle, *Case for Healing*, 80.
79. Sawvelle, *Case for Healing*, 80.
80. MacNutt, *Healing Reawakening*, 80.
81. MacNutt, *Healing Reawakening*, 80.
82. MacNutt, *Healing Reawakening*, 80.

The Importance of IHD for Effective Discipleship

Kelsey writes that with the establishment of the Byzantine Empire, the Christian church emerged from the underground and became one of the most important Byzantine institutions. Athanasius (296–393 AD), the Bishop of Alexandria in Egypt during the fourth century, accepted the doctrine endorsed at the Council of Nicea in 325 AD that Christ was both man and God and that He gave His saints His power to do His works of healing.[83] During this period, four other great bishops in the Eastern Orthodox Church, wrote of their theology, which included within it, the practice of healing in the church. These four bishops were Basil the Great (329–379 AD), his brother Gregory of Nyssa (331–396 AD), their friend Gregory of Nazianzus (329–389 AD), and John Chrysostom (345–407 AD).[84]

In the West, although healings were recorded by the saintly Ambrose (340–397 AD), Augustine of Hippo (354–430), Jerome (340–420 AD), Gregory the Great (540 AD–early part of the seventh century), Sulpitious Severus (363–425AD), the biographer of St Martin of Tours, and John Cassian (360–435AD) (whose thoughts influenced Western monasticism), the view on healing took a distinctly different angle that eventually led to the diminishing of healing in the ministry life of the church.[85]

These men's acceptance of Plato's worldview, which emphasized the interaction of the physical and non-physical worlds, helped bolster the acceptance of spiritual healing.[86] They believed that humans suffer from physical and mental illness because of the work of demons on the totality of the human mind. Christ's crucifixion and resurrection were accepted as the work of God that defeated every demonic spirit, and the spirit-filled Christian had the same power of Christ to defeat demonic attacks and bring healing to the mind.[87] Inspite of this, they diminished the importance of healing; this was a major sign of the beginning of the decline of the healing ministry of the church.

Sawvelle asserts that by the fifth century, Augustine, bishop of Hippo a significantly influential Christian Theologian, started a theological position that expressly denied the workings of healing and miracles in his lifetime.[88] Augustine wrote that miracles must not be allowed to continue, to prevent

---

83. Porterfield, *Healing in the History*, 64.
84. Kelsey, *Healing and Christianity*, 127.
85. Kelsey, *Healing and Christianity*, 127.
86. Kelsey, *Healing and Christianity*, 110–18.
87. Kelsey, *Healing and Christianity*, 128.
88. Sawvelle, *A Case for Healing*, 82.

believers from being dependent on visible signs and experiences.[89] Towards the completion of his work *The City of God* however, Augustine shifted his cessationist position in favor of the ministry of healing and deliverance. He wrote that he had not had enough time to record all the miracles, similar to biblical records and earlier times of church history, that he had witnessed.[90]

Augustine's subsequent repudiation of his previous cessationist position did not however, stop the diminishing of the healing and deliverance practice—his former view had already done its damage. He complained that many miracles were not known because the communication about miracles had been suppressed by the unbelief of many people.[91] Similarly, Jerome, whose contribution was the *Vulgate,* also turned believers' focus away from actual real healing to acts of healing that were symbolic.[92] John Cassian's discussion on healing entailed putting forth the idea that there were specific perceived dangers of using the gifts of healing, which include losing one's humility, inward purity and perfect chastity—tantamount to losing one's soul for concentrating on healing human sickness.[93]

Gregory the Great's emphasis was on sickness as an instrument of God in bringing correction and repentance to a person to bring transformation for eternity.[94] Hence, while he did not deny the possibility of healing, he was more focused on God's will to heal.[95] The church in the West had begun making decisions to limit the ministry of healing, setting boundaries that would continue to diminish the operations of the gifts of the Holy Spirit as she entered into its Medieval years. It became increasingly obvious that man's opinion was defining the will of God—that is, man had decided that God was not going to do any more miracles, and that healing had only a symbolic (not a literal) meaning.

THE MIDDLE AGES (500–1500 AD)

At the end of the fifth century, which was the beginning of the Middle Ages (inclusive of the Medieval Ages at its beginning), the Roman Empire

89. Kelsey, *Healing and Christianity,* 146.
90. Augustine, "*City of God,* Book 22.8."
91. Sawvelle, *Case for Healing,* 80.
92. Kelsey, *Healing and Christianity,* 152.
93. Kelsey, *Healing and Christianity,* 153.
94. Kelsey, *Healing and Christianity,* 154.
95. Kelsey, *Healing and Christianity,* 155.

The Importance of IHD for Effective Discipleship

collapsed.[96] Politically, Europe was seized by feudalism with turmoil of wars between feudal lords and kings. This was "a time of widespread wars, accompanied by a general lack of learning", resulting in the obscurity of many central truths of Christianity.[97] In addition, prayer for healing became relegated to the clergy instead of the prerogative of every believer, as was the case in the early church.

This period saw a change of emphasis from "this life" to the next, as chaos took place with the collapse of educational systems, with cities emptying out, and with disease, depression and despair taking center stage.[98] The word "healed" was sometimes translated as "saved", as Scripture was translated to Latin, which led also to changes in practices in the Catholic Church, such that "the anointing to heal became known as the 'Extreme Unction for Dying.'"[99] Sawvelle writes that the use of anointing oil and prayer for healing the sick was changed to a final act of preparation for death—an assurance of entering heaven without visiting purgatory.[100]

During this era of church history, a foundation was being laid for a movement away from the first century healing ministry of the church. Influential bishops such as Gregory the Great (540–604 AD) adopted a cessationist position that acknowledged the need for miracles for the growth and establishment of the church at the point of the birth of the church, but which was no longer necessary as the church became established.[101] In addition, the church took a rational approach to its doctrine and by way of reasoning, reduced the significance of healing.[102] What became predominant according to Ruthven, is that many church leaders began to subscribe to the belief that Christians were no longer to seek or desire after miracles, but instead, were to pay attention to living their lives according to the values and principles found in the bible and in church doctrines.[103]

Europe in the sixth and seventh centuries also saw disasters and plagues sweeping across the continent. Expectations of healing miracles morphed into a resigned acceptance that sickness was no longer seen as an

---

96. MacNutt, *Healing Reawakening*, 118.
97. MacNutt, *Healing Reawakening*, 121.
98. Clark, *Biblical Guidebook*, 34–35.
99. Clark, *Biblical Guidebook*, 36.
100. Sawvelle, *Case for Healing*, 88.
101. Sawvelle, *Case for Healing*, 87.
102. Clark, *Biblical Guidebook*, 38.
103. Sawvelle, *Case for Healing*, 86.

opportunity for God to manifest His love nor His desire to heal, as seen in the life ministry of Jesus and His disciples.[104] Instead, illness was to be interpreted as a remedial and corrective act of God with the use of pain-inflicting powers divinely approved, to bring moral restoration to mankind.[105]

The shifting in this period notwithstanding, miracles of healings were recorded by Gregory the Great himself, who documented healings and miracles performed through Benedict in His Dialogues; by Charles the Archbishop of Glasglow contemplating Cuthbert's prayer that brought healing for many; by the saintly John of Beverly, the bishop of York; and by Saint Hospicus.[106] According to Craig S. Keener, both medieval Western and Eastern churches recorded healings taking place.[107] However, many of these records included healings that accompanied veneration of the miraculous powers of the saints. People revered their bones, graves and relics. Potterfield observes that these physical tokens became seen as another acceptable approach to access the healing powers of godly man in their absence.[108] In addition to icons, there were also many healing shrines that were built. Sacraments such as penance, baptism, and Eucharist became channels and forms of healing.[109] Keener says that uneducated Christians felt able to connect with past eras of God's working through these.[110] The practice of healing was no longer the same as in the days of Jesus and the early years of the church, which was ministered by ordinary Christians through the power of the Holy Spirit in the name of Jesus.

This period also saw the rise of the monastic movement led by "Desert Fathers" who established themselves in the deserts of Northern Africa in pursuit of holiness that was declining within the main body of the church.[111] Cardinal Leon Joseph Suenens considered the monastic movement as a charismatic movement with miraculous gifts of the Holy Spirit being evident among the monastics. They continued to practise healing and deliverance and gained notoriety for it.[112] The miraculous gifts of the Holy Spirit,

---

104. Sawvelle, *Case for Healing*, 87.
105. Kelsey, *Healing and Christianity*, 155.
106. Sawvelle, *Case for Healing*, 91.
107. Keener, *Miracles*, 368–71.
108. Porterfield, *Healing in the History*, 76.
109. Porterfield, *Healing in the History*, 69–90.
110. Keener, *Miracles*, 1:369.
111. Clark, *Biblical Guidebook*, 36.
112. Clark, *Biblical Guidebook*, 37.

The Importance of IHD for Effective Discipleship

which disappeared from the institutional church, now appeared among the monastics.

Another important shift in Christian theology took place in Christendom with Aristotle's philosophy replacing Plato in explaining life. Kelsey wrote that by the fifth century, people were separating themselves from the Greek culture and reading Greek text became a dying art, learnt only by a few. By 1054, Latin became the principal language. Plato's work was history, and Aristotle's work dominated.[113]

The Platonian framework of philosophy provides "a carefully expressed notion of a non-physical and eternal world which shapes and directs the physical world."[114] Plato's idea is that there is a constant and continuous interaction between the participants (human beings) in the physical world, with the participants of the spiritual realm of spirits, demons, deities and ideas.[115] Kelsey asserts that in this worldview, there was full support for the belief that there is an interaction that goes on between man and God through dreams, visions, prophecies, angels and demons as described in the Old and New Testaments.[116] He calls Plato "the philosopher of Shamanistic experience"—man's attempt to connect with both the physical and spiritual worlds.[117]

In contrast to Plato, Aristotle's worldview is that all knowledge of man is gained through logic and reasoning, as we experience life with our senses.[118] Kelsey's conclusion on Aristotle is that our knowledge is the result of first experiences in our senses and then reasoning creates the knowledge as person mature in their thinking.[119]

For Aristotle, the gathering of information begins with sense experience, and can only be accepted as absolute knowledge upon first verification by way of deductive reasoning, not inductive reasoning. He did not consider information from sense experience or processed information through inductive reasoning to be definitive knowledge, as these are still changeable. Hence, any knowledge can only be accepted as final or absolute when it comes through deductive reasoning. Kelsey says that Aristotle

---

113. Kelsey, *Encounter with God*, 62.
114. Kelsey, *Healing and Christianity*, 111.
115. Kelsey, *Healing and Christianity*, 111.
116. Kelsey, *Healing and Christianity*, 111.
117. Kelsey, *Healing and Christianity*, 111.
118. Kelsey, *Encounter with God*, 64.
119. Kelsey, *Encounter with God*, 65.

Where Might God be Placing the IHD Ministry?

leaned considerably more to deductive reasoning (which he felt more certain of), rather than inductive thinking, to find absolute knowledge about things around us.[120] Aristotle believed that knowledge of the ultimate reality or of God, cannot be obtained through divine inspiration but by human rational activity.[121] In divine inspiration, he included dreams, visions and any direct supernatural interactions.[122]

Thomas Aquinas (1225–1274), an Italian Dominican theologian, introduced what was known as Aquinas-Aristotelian synthesis.[123] Here he integrated Christian thought with Aristotelian philosophy and shifted Christendom away from Plato's philosophy. Kelsey says that theology followed the ideas of Aristotle and ended up creating a huge divide between God and human beings with no channels for communication and little room for miracles.[124]

Kelsey says that Aquinas concluded that Christians must accept this as doctrinal truths.[125] Aquinas took Aristotle's position that the knowledge of God is only derived logically, and not from any experience of dreams, visions, healing or any supernatural encounters.[126] While he did not deny the possibility of supernatural knowledge, he explained that these were deliberate specific revelations, namely that God had chosen to reveal Himself in Christ Jesus that was beyond human reason.[127] According to Kelsey, Barth holds a similar position with Aquinas. Barth makes the point that God broke into man's world only once historically through Jesus Christ, with many supernatural deeds and manifestations, so that man might know God. After that, man should have no expectation of God's further supernatural intrusion because there are no natural means and process that exist for regular interaction between God and man.[128] Unlike Barth, Aquinas permitted room for the supernatural, which he himself experienced.[129]

---

120. Kelsey, *Encounter with God*, 65.
121. Kelsey, *Encounter with God*, 65.
122. Kelsey, *Encounter with God*, 65.
123. Clark, *Biblical Guidebook*, 38.
124. Kelsey, *Healing and Christianity*, 158.
125. Kelsey, *Encounter with God*, 64.
126. Kelsey, *Encounter with God*, 65.
127. Kelsey, *Encounter with God*, 66.
128. Kelsey, *Encounter with God*, 66.
129. Kelsey, *Encounter with God*, 66.

The Importance of IHD for Effective Discipleship

This theology moved the church further away from the first-century healing paradigm gradually phased out by Aristotelian philosophy.[130] The impact of this was that it made it difficult for the church to allow God to have direct access to heal and transform lives through the power of the Holy Spirit. The integrated discipleship methodology of Jesus through His teaching, power and acts of healing that saw the transformation of lives, was gradually shut out of the church. Discipleship steered away from the miraculous and supernatural works of God, towards intellectual engagement with scripture, thinking, deductive reasoning, logic and interaction with the physical world. This was to continue into the years of the Reformation and Modernity.

REFORMATION ONWARDS: PUTTING TO DEATH DIVINE HEALING

The Reformation years started in 1517 when Martin Luther posted his Ninety-Five Theses on the door of the church in Wittenberg. The Protestant movement headed by Luther, Calvin, Zwingli, and other Reformers was an act of bringing the church back "to an adherence of scripture alone, *sola scriptura*, by grace alone, *sola gratia*, by faith alone, *sola fide*, and by Christ alone, *sola Christi*."[131]

One major focus of this movement was a reaction to the abusive practices of the church such as trafficking in inauthentic relics, cult of the saints, inauthentic miracle claims, and Catholic apologetics.[132] By the time of the Reformers, healing miracles had drifted so far from how they were manifested through Jesus and His disciples, that they were now being relegated to miracle shrines, relics and saints. Each saint had a special area of help for man—"St. Apollo for toothache, St. Roch for plague, St. Christopher for protection against sudden death."[133] The reformers took a theological position to reject and oppose the miraculous and the healing and deliverance aspects of the gospel.[134]

Martin Luther, a leading proponent of Protestantism has often been characterized as anti-miraculous. Randy Clark asserts that this was not

---

130. Clark, *Biblical Guidebook*, 38.
131. Sawvelle, *Case for Healing*, 95.
132. Keener, *Miracles*, 1:371–75.
133. Porterfield, *Healing in the History*, 94.
134. Sawvelle, *Case for Healing*, 95.

Where Might God be Placing the IHD Ministry?

true and he quotes Luther: "How often has it happened, and still does, that devils have been driven out in the name of Christ; also by calling on His name and prayer, the sick have been healed."[135] Luther himself witnessed the deliverance of a girl from demonic spirits after he prayed for her, and the healing of his good friend Philip Melancthon, who was near death.[136] According to Keener, Luther taught on how to pray for the sick (James 5:14-15) in many places. It is said that in a letter he scribbled: "prayer for healing by the laying on of hands occurring in Wittenberg."[137] However, Luther did take the position that it was no longer necessary for God to work in the ordinary physical world as He did once, through Jesus and during the Apostolic Era.[138]

The theologian of the Reformation who dealt the greatest death blow to the subject of healing during the time of the reformers, was the French Reformer John Calvin (1509–1564).[139] John Calvin was among those who radically challenged the validity of healing miracles. He expressed absolute disapproval for appeals of healing miracles to saints, calling them sinful practices, and wrote instructions on how to worship a God who is beyond human reach.[140] To Calvin, God is absolutely transcendent and it is impossible for finite nature to host a God who is infinitely immense. He insisted that the miraculous does not occur in our daily living in the physical world, and that things that are miraculous are God-given exceptions, not normalities.[141] He took an extreme position, dismissing the gifts of healing and interpretation as temporary, and even removed healing from the list of Christian ministries.[142] To Calvin, supernatural gifts were only given to Christ's early disciples to testify of the reality of Christ's life on earth, and were never intended to be applied in the normal practices of Christian living.[143] He believed that the death of the last Apostle signaled the end of all miracles.[144] MacNutt says that Calvin converted cessationism into

---

135. Clark, *Biblical Guide*, 39.
136. Sawvelle, *Case for Healing*, 99–101.
137. Keener, *Miracles*, 1:373.
138. Kelsey, *Healing and Christianity*, 174.
139. MacNutt, *Healing Reawakening*, 140.
140. Porterfield, *Healing in the History*, 95.
141. Porterfield, *Healing in the History*, 96–98.
142. Porterfield, *Healing in the History*, 95.
143. Porterfield, *Healing in the History*, 95.
144. MacNutt, *Healing Reawakening*, 140.

The Importance of IHD for Effective Discipleship

basic doctrine.[145] In addition, Calvin believed and taught that after the resurrection, all demonic spirits were expelled from this world, and he called for the dismantling and ending of all healing ministry, inclusive of exorcism by all Christians.[146] Calvin's position is largely the result of him having seen only the abuses of the healing ministry, as practised in Europe during his time.[147]

Another important damage to the healing ministry after Calvin, came at the hand of David Hume (1711–1776). Hume was a Scottish philosopher from the school of Scottish realism, science and religion, and was a very well received philosopher whom many listened to, during the eighteenth century Enlightenment period that highly regarded human thinking and reasoning.[148] Hume declared that there were never any miracles performed by Jesus.[149] According to MacNutt, Hume's writing, *An Enquiry Concerning Human Understanding*, obliterated the idea of miracles completely, from the European Humanistic worldview.[150]

This was a period where science and religion were headed in different directions, and the educated was persuaded and taught by scientific materialism to only consider as certainty or reality, what could be seen and measured.[151] Hence, angels, demons, and miraculous healing became myths to the educated class and the liberal wing of Protestantism.[152] Protestantism had divided into two wings—"the 'conservatives' whose position is that all signs and wonders stopped nineteen hundred years ago; and the 'liberals' who claim that miracles never took place at all. These are still the two divides amongst Protestant Christians, affecting how they live out their faith.[153] According to MacNutt, the "ordinary Christians," who were less highly educated, held onto the literal understanding of the Bible, but the professors and ministers, succumbing to a secular scientific worldview, saw healing and exorcism as a worldview of the uneducated, stemming from

---

145. MacNutt, *Healing Reawakening*, 140.
146. MacNutt, *Healing Reawakening*, 149.
147. MacNutt, *Healing Reawakening*, 141.
148. MacNutt, *Healing Reawakening*, 145.
149. MacNutt, *Healing Reawakening*, 145.
150. MacNutt, *Healing Reawakening*, 146.
151. MacNutt, *Healing Reawakening*, 146.
152. MacNutt, *Healing Reawakening*, 146.
153. MacNutt, *Healing Reawakening*, 146.

Where Might God be Placing the IHD Ministry?

an antiquated ideology that educated people cannot accept.[154] An example is William Barclay, the popular Scottish theologian, who wrote *The Daily Study Bible Series*. He implied that "Jesus simply used the power of suggestion when He cast out evil spirits."[155] Barclay was of the opinion that people experienced healing from deliverance because they were under the delusion that they were demon-possessed, and therefore exhibited the symptoms of demon-possession, which were then easily resolved or healed through exorcism.[156] He suggested that this was the case in the Eastern world where all illness was ascribed to the malignant power of demons and devils.[157]

John Nelson Darby (1800–1882) was another theologian who had a role in setting back the healing ministry. Darby dropped Anglicanism to join the Plymouth Brethren and became the Brethren's most influential theologian.[158] One of his theories among several that influenced the conservative wing of evangelical Christianity was dispensationalism.[159] Dispensationalism claims that the historical time line of the church is segmented into several periods or "dispensations".[160] According to Darby, healing miracles and the gifts of the Holy Spirit (1 Cor 12) was God's plan for the dispensation of the Apostles.[161] He took the same position as Calvin believing that healing and other charismatic gifts ended with the death of the last apostle.[162] MacNutt believes that Darby's teachings had effectively sealed the door on healing prayer, to the conservative evangelical wing of Protestants.[163]

According to Kelsey, two major theologians, Karl Barth (one of the most significant theologians for the more fundamentalist and orthodox believers), and Rudolph Bultmann (a most influential New Testament theologian for liberal believers), pushed God's power to love and care for the created world, further away.[164] Barth said that miracle healings are "a

---

154. MacNutt, *Healing Reawakening*, 147.
155. MacNutt, *Healing Reawakening*, 147.
156. Barclay, *Gospel of Matthew*, v.
157. Barclay, *Gospel of Matthew*, v.
158. MacNutt, *Healing Reawakening*, 148.
159. MacNutt, *Healing Reawakening*, 148.
160. MacNutt, *Healing Reawakening*, 148.
161. MacNutt, *Healing Reawakening*, 148–49.
162. MacNutt, *Healing Reawakening*, 148.
163. MacNutt, *Healing Reawakening*, 150.
164. Kelsey, *Healing and Christianity*, 176.

The Importance of IHD for Effective Discipleship

thing of the past" that no longer happen. Bultmann's assertion is that all New Testament miracles never happened.[165]

Bultmann (1884–1976) strengthened the case against healing for liberal and existential theology, declaring that healing never took place even during the time of Jesus, and maintaining the liberal position that the miracle stories of the gospels were "myths."[166] His basic argument was that God has no influence in our world that is not accessible to Him, and that all signs and wonders and even the resurrection itself were myths that are not acceptable in modern worldview.[167] Bultmann was totally hostile to the ministry of healing and deliverance and assessed Johann Christopher Blumhardt's (a Lutheran pastor) ministry of healing and deliverance as "legend" and "abomination."[168] According to MacNutt, many prominent professors at German universities were Bultmann's students who had in fact taken over many Protestant seminaries run by liberals.[169] The result was that the most educated Protestants and clergies were absolutely closed to the subject of healing and deliverance.[170] Dietrich Bonhoeffer took similar positions alongside Barth and Bultmann. He wrote in *Letters from Prison*, that man has matured in his understanding and is able to govern the physical world effectively, and no one needs a God to help, as man is no longer helpless.[171]

TWENTIETH CENTURY RE-EMERGENCE OF DIVINE HEALING FROM THE EMBERS

Although the intellectual educated world of Christianity had taken a position against God's involvement in the transformation of human lives through His power by acts of healing and miracles, healing by the power of God still continued to occur. Records of miraculous healings exist from after the Reformation years. Martin Luther (1483–1546) himself witnessed the healing of his friend Melanchton, as Luther prayed for him.[172] George Fox (1624–1691), founder of the Society of Friends, left behind an

165. Kelsey, *Healing and Christianity*, 176–77.
166. MacNutt, *Healing Reawakening*, 151.
167. MacNutt, *Healing Reawakening*, 151.
168. MacNutt, *Healing Reawakening*, 152.
169. MacNutt, *Healing Reawakening*, 152.
170. MacNutt, *Healing Reawakening*, 152.
171. Kelsey, *Healing and Christianity*, 177.
172. Woolmer, *Healing and Deliverance*, 176.

Where Might God be Placing the IHD Ministry?

unpublished bounded manuscript, referred to as *Book of Miracles*, which contains his records of concrete facts relating to miracles.[173] Richard Baxter (1615–1691), one of the great Puritan leaders, recorded a healing from a tumor he had.[174] Count Zinzendorf (1700–1760), one of the leaders of the Moravians, testified that they had witnessed the healing acts of God against incurable maladies such as cancer.[175] John Wesley (1703–1791) described many miracles of God's healing through his prayer for the sick, including the healing that came upon his horse as he prayed for his horse.[176] J.C. Blumhart (1805–1880), a Lutheran pastor, was known for his healing ministry at a *Kurhaus* (healing center) that he founded.[177] Others who saw evidences of the power of God included Jonathan Edwards, whose preaching started a famous revival in Northampton, Massachusetts in 1734, and George Whitefield, an Anglican preacher who in 1739 stirred up what is referred to as the Great Awakening in the American colonies.[178] According to Kelsey, both revivals, which saw the move of the Holy Spirit, were blocked by the institutional church, due partly to doctrinal reasons and partly to excesses and aberrations that gave the revivals a bad name.[179] Other early healing practices documented in Paul Chappell's research include Mother Ann Lee and the Shakers, John Humphrey Noyes and the Oneida Community, and Ellen G. White and the Adventists.[180] European contributors to Divine Healing named by Chappell include Edward Irving, Johann Blumhart, Dorothea Trudel, Samweul Zeller, and Otto Stockmayer.[181]

According to William De Arteaga, whilst the doctrine of cessationism reached its height in the Nineteenth Century, revival was happening in England, South Africa, India and the United States, with signs and wonders following—God was showing His presence and power.[182] Most of these revivals were part of the Holiness Movement in America prior to the mid-nineteenth century. These revivals were carried by a gathering of

---

173. Kelsey, *Healing and Christianity*, 132.
174. Woolmer, *Healing and Deliverance*, 180.
175. Woolmer, *Healing and Deliverance*, 180.
176. Kelsey, *Healing and Christianity*, 184.
177. Woolmer, *Healing and Deliverance*, 184.
178. MacNutt, *Healing Reawakening*, 171–76.
179. Kelsey, *Healing and Christianity*, 174–75.
180. Alexander, *Pentecostal Healing*, 3.
181. Alexander, *Pentecostal Healing*, 3.
182. Sawvelle, *Case for Healing*, 108.

The Importance of IHD for Effective Discipleship

Christians from different denominations who embraced the doctrine of 'entire sanctification', and seeing the move of the Holy Spirit with power.[183] Its theology was anchored on the theology and practice of John Wesley, Church of England minister, founder of Methodism, and father of the Wesleyan Holiness, who pursued with all fervency the commandment to be perfect as God the Heavenly Father, is perfect. He believed that a person could become "perfect in love or intention in this life."[184]

Emerging out of the Holiness Movement was the parallel rise of the healing theology.[185] Kelsey says that in the later years of the nineteenth century, this renewed pursuit of the divine healing was happening in Europe and America and mostly amongst the common people, outside of the established churches.[186] The theological focus of this new healing movement was that healing was in the Atonement, just as salvation from sin was available to all in the Atonement.[187] According to De Arteaga, the most popular name for the movement was the Faith Cure Movement, although there were other names such as Divine Healing movement or Evangelical Healing Movement. The focus of this revival was healing through targeted prayer focus on healing.[188]

Paul Chappell identified this movement as a gathering of Christians with a fervent belief, and the pursuit of a God, who heals physical disease and illness by His power, as they prayed in faith.[189] Kimberley Alexander defined it as ". . . that Christian movement which maintains a belief that physical disease or illness can be cured or healed by God's supernatural intervention, when the prayer of faith is prayed; this healing is available as part of salvation."[190] According to Chappell, the pioneers of this movement include Ethan Allen, Sarah and Edward Mix, Charles Cullis, William Boardman, A.J. Gordon, Andrew Murray, A.B. Simpson, Carrie Judd Montgomery, and Alexander Dowie.[191]

---

183. Stephens, *Who Healeth All*, 11.
184. Hardesty, *Faith Cure*, 27.
185. Alexander, *Pentecostal Healing*, 3.
186. Kelsey, *Healing and Christianity*, 185.
187. Keener, *Miracles*, 1:390.
188. Sawvelle, *Case for Healing*, 110.
189. Chappell, "Divine Healing Movement," 9.
190. Alexander, *Pentecostal Healing*, 9.
191. Chappell, "Divine Healing Movement," 3.

Where Might God be Placing the IHD Ministry?

Charles Cullis of Boston (1833–1892), an Episcopalian, is considered as the Father of the Divine Healing Movement.[192] Cullis began as a homeopathic physician who believed that God had called him to care for the sick. In the late 1860's Cullis' contemplation of Jas 5:14, 15 led him to incorporate prayer of faith in his care for the sick.[193] In 1879, Cullis announced that hundreds had been healed as a result of this practice.[194] Cullis believed that healing was provided in the Atonement as was salvation, and he convinced others in the Holiness movement such as James Inkip, W.E. Broadman and Daniel Steele.[195] He published *Cullis's Annual Report of the Consumptives' Home* which contained testimonies of healing. He also opened a faith cure home in Boston.[196]

Another Bostonian who played a major part in advancing the doctrine of divine healing was A.J. Gordon, a Baptist pastor. Gordon, who was a trustee of Cullis' faith work, witnessed the instantaneous healing of an opium addict, and of a missionary with a cancerous jaw in 1877 at D.L. Moody's meeting in Boston.[197] After seriously studying scriptures on divine healing, he published an influential tract in 1881 entitled, "The Ministry of Healing—Miracles of Cure in All Ages." [198] He defended healing on two fronts—against the cessationists, and criticized Mary Baker Eddy and Christian Science "as being neither Christian nor scientific."[199]

Another major force in the advancement of the healing movement was provided by A.B. Simpson, who founded the Christian and Missionary Alliance.[200] Simpson's influences included Frank Sandford, Charles Parham, and Carrie Judd, with some even guessing that Aimee Semple MacPherson's Foursquare Gospel was a make-over of Simpson's Four-Fold Gospel.[201]

It was after 1880 when Simpson attended Cullis' faith convention, after suffering a complete physical and nervous breakdown, that he became

192. Alexander, *Pentecostal Healing*, 16.
193. Alexander, *Pentecostal Healing*, 16.
194. Alexander, *Pentecostal Healing*, 16.
195. Alexander, *Pentecostal Healing*, 17.
196. Alexander, *Pentecostal Healing*, 17.
197. Alexander, *Pentecostal Healing*, 18–19.
198. Alexander, *Pentecostal Healing*, 19.
199. MacNutt, *Healing Reawakening*, 178.
200. Alexander, *Pentecostal Healing*, 19.
201. Alexander, *Pentecostal Healing*, 19.

The Importance of IHD for Effective Discipleship

open to the doctrine of divine healing, experiencing healing for himself.[202] Simpson came to the conclusion, after much study of scripture, that Christ's atonement has removed sin and its effect on every believer; and healing is a benefit of the completed work of Christ for all who accept the Lordship of Jesus."[203] Simpson believed that healing was the redemptive right of believers in every era.[204] He resigned from his Presbyterian pastorate and founded the nondenominational Gospel Tabernacle (1882) and the Berachah Home for healing (1883) in New York City.[205] According to Heather Curtis, Simpson challenged the conviction that "glory . . . rebounds to God for our submission to His will in sickness and the happy results of sanctification affection."[206]

Simpson took many of Rev D. D. Smith Wilmington's position on why God was reviving the healing ministry.[207] These included firstly, God making man whole to prove God is a real, personal Being, and that Christ is the Redeemer of the soul and the body; secondly, that prayer is a power, a force, and an answer; thirdly, so that believers can be brought into the ministry—as they experienced healing through prayer; fourthly, to gather the saints together to establish the Kingdom of God; fifthly, as an alternative to dependency and indulgence in material gains and wants; sixthly, the winning of souls because of the soon coming return of Christ; and finally, the testimonies of those who had been healed confronted those who mock Christianity and its belief in God.[208] Simpson was regarded by many as "the forerunner of Pentecostal theology, noted for a hermeneutical method which derived truth or doctrine from biblical narrative, primarily the narrative of the book of Acts."[209]

In the last third of the nineteenth century, the divine healing movement in the United States grew, with many camp meetings and conventions.[210] Charles Cullis' first "faith convention" was held in 1874 in Framingham, Massachusetts, followed by weeklong meetings at the

---

202. Alexander, *Pentecostal Healing*, 20.
203. Brown, *Global Pentecostal and Charismatic Healing*, 35.
204. Brown, *Global Pentecostal and Charismatic Healing*, 35.
205. Brown, *Global Pentecostal and Charismatic Healing*, 35.
206. Brown, *Global Pentecostal and Charismatic Healing*, 35.
207. Brown, *Global Pentecostal and Charismatic Healing*, 34.
208. Brown, *Global Pentecostal and Charismatic Healing*, 34–36.
209. Alexander, *Pentecostal Healing*, 22.
210. Hardesty, *Faith Cure*, 41.

Where Might God be Placing the IHD Ministry?

Methodists' Old Orchard, Maine campgrounds between 876–1883.[211] Simpson held a "Convention for Christian Life, Divine Healing and Evangelistic and Missionary Work" in 1884 at the New York Gospel Tabernacle.[212] He and his colleagues promoted these road-show faith-cure meetings—to Philadelphia, Pittsburg, Buffalo (1885), Chicago (1889), Detroit, Kansas City (1895), Atlanta (1899), Toronto (1891), and Los Angeles (1895). Such faith-cure conventions were used to spread the word on salvation and healing. In addition to these camp meetings and faith conventions, several of its major proponents started healing homes dedicated to praying for healing. These included Carrie Judd's Faith Rest Cottage, A.B. Simpson's Berachah Home, Mrs. Baxter's Bethshan, and Alexander Dowie's healing homes in Chicago.[213] According to Curtis, divine healing had spread from Switzerland and Germany across Europe and to Great Britain, the United States, Australia, and India by 1885.[214]

MacNutt wrote that while these holiness and healing revival meetings of the eighteenth and nineteenth centuries saw massive repentance, healings, and signs and wonders, and changed lives, it was still mostly the uneducated, marginalized people who were responding. Those in establishments such as the Congregationalists and the Episcopalians dismissed these events as "emotional, hysterical outbursts of ignorant people, 'hillbillies.'"[215] MacNutt's summary of the nineteenth century is that there were many sporadic instances of leaders of churches experiencing the touch of God; whilst the official authority remained totally closed up to God's attempt to touch His church. By the time of the twentieth century, God had started a wave of awakenings to His presence and His power seemingly to make a definite point of His presence and His desire to be a part of His church.[216]

Up to this point, the importance of the healing and deliverance ministry of Jesus for the transformation of lives had yet to be fully accepted, understood and realized, although God brought many into encounter with His healing grace.

Breaking into the scene in the twentieth century, was the Pentecostal Movement that saw the release of the power of God and the beginnings of a

---

211. Hardesty, *Faith Cure*, 41.
212. Hardesty, *Faith Cure*, 44.
213. Hardesty, *Faith Cure*, 57.
214. Brown, *Global Pentecostal and Charismatic Healing*, 33.
215. MacNutt, *Healing Reawakening*, 188.
216. MacNutt, *Healing Reawakening*, 188.

The Importance of IHD for Effective Discipleship

new era of signs and wonders, miracles and healings. The explosiveness of the Pentecostal revival could not be contained and began to spread rapidly. Thirty eight missionaries were sent out within six months of the founding of the Azusa missions to major cities of the United States and the spread went on further to Egypt, Norway and Africa.[217] Harvey Cox observed that Christianity continued with Pentecost breaking free from traditionalism, scientism, creed, and abolishing hierarchies, but keeping the ecstasy of a personal experience with God that transforms. Meanwhile, the religious conservatives stayed rooted in their established doctrines and hierarchy while the liberals continued to remain socially relevant.[218]

MacNutt points out that Pentecostalism differentiated itself from established Christian denominations through the experience of the power of Christ's ministry by the works of the Holy Spirit, as opposed to focusing only on the teachings and practices that were symbolic of the presence of the unseen God (e.g., sacrament)[219] He elaborates that Pentecostals taught Christians to have an expectation of healing and deliverance through prayer because God was wanting to remove obstacles obstructing believers from a relationship with Him[220] MacNutt further states that Pentecostalism is about God personally at work to change people's lives.[221] He rightly analyses that Pentecostal preachers encouraged listeners to expect God to impact and change their lives in extraordinary ways.[222] It is this openness to a God encounter that leads to a dramatic experiential transformation of lives by the Holy Spirit, which deepens faith and creates a hunger for a pursuit after the will of God. MacNutt wrote that Christians who experienced the Person of Christ, alive and real, continued to encounter the power of God with the activation of all the charismatic gifts. People's encounter with Christ continued with the activation of all the gifts of the Holy Spirit that healed their lives and freed people from sickness, addictions, emotional disorders and demonic spirits to a significant degree, enabling them to experience living the abundant life to a greater degree, even as they continued to encounter sufferings from living in a fallen world. They encountered the love of God the Father, and of Jesus, and discovered intimacy with a loving

---

217. MacNutt, *Healing Reawakening*, 194.
218. MacNutt, *Healing Reawakening*, 194.
219. MacNutt, *Healing Reawakening*, 194.
220. MacNutt, *Healing Reawakening*, 194–95.
221. MacNutt, *Healing Reawakening*, 195.
222. MacNutt, *Healing Reawakening*, 195.

God instead of a Magistrate of Heaven or a transcendent inaccessible God of antiquity who is unreachable.[223]

Early Pentecostals were zealous in promoting the belief that Christ's death by crucifixion, as an atonement for sin, had also secured healing for man.[224] F.M. Britton, a former leader in the Fire-Baptized Holiness Church said that the atonement was complete in providing for the pardon for sin and the washing from all unrighteousness, so that healing is secured in the atonement appropriated by faith.[225] There was a single-minded focus on the centrality of faith in the actualization of healing from God. A quote from a 1926 issue of Golden Grain, a periodical published by healing evangelist Charles Price said that there are no "maybes" in the prayer of faith, and that God will only hear prayers of faith, not doubt. God meant it and so He commanded it, telling the church leaders to pray in faith and let Him perform the healing.[226]

Early Pentecostals had a strong emphasis on spiritual warfare as part of the healing process and an absolute prohibition against seeking medical aid. The nineteenth century Evangelicals who promoted healing did not however share the same view on the issue of deliverance from demonic powers.[227] For the Pentecostals, the number one enemy in the war of health was Satan, who was out to destroy the human body and mind and this involved a spiritual battle. A commentator articulated in the *Apostolic Faith* in 1907: "Every sickness is of the devil."[228] Hence deliverance played a key role in the healing process.

Many early Pentecostals took a firm stand against medical practices, which at the time, was a poorly developed science anyway.[229] Dowie popularized the view that science is the only accurate knowledge, not medicine which is a "guess", and not a science.[230] Many early Pentecostals rejected medical science but not general science and frequently praised the advancements that were made in technological science.

---

223. MacNutt, *Healing Reawakening*, 207.
224. Williams, *Spirit Cure*, 26.
225. Williams, *Spirit Cure*, 26.
226. Williams, *Spirit Cure*, 26.
227. Williams, *Spirit Cure*, 28.
228. Williams, *Spirit Cure*, 29.
229. Williams, *Spirit Cure*, 30–34.
230. Williams, *Spirit Cure*, 34.

The Importance of IHD for Effective Discipleship

As time progressed, Pentecostals became less objectionable towards medical assistance. By mid-century, with the growing prestige and success of medical establishments, Pentecostals found it difficult to discount claims regarding the healing science of medicine.[231] In 1949, a major figure contributing to the Pentecostal healing ministry, Oral Roberts "admitted that there were instances when 'nature has not been weakened beyond its power to resist disease,' in which case the body responds to medical treatment since doctors can assist nature."[232] Roberts further said in 1957 that he believed that good doctors are given by God because wellness is God's intent for man. Roberts says that man must do everything he can for himself, and whatever is beyond mortal man to do, is left to the work of God according to His promises.[233]

Healing evangelists such as Roberts carved out a role for doctors while focusing on God as the primary Healer.

During the 1960s and 70s, Kathryn Kuhlman was a major proponent of the healing ministry within the charismatic movement.[234] With regards to doctors, Kathryn showed acceptance of their role, affirmed the validity of modern medicine, yet criticized their proneness to discounting the miraculous. She is reported to have said that she supported the wonderful works of doctors bringing cure to man, but that she stood firmly in her belief that the Holy Spirit cures.[235]

While the divine healing movement made relationship bridges and connections with doctors, relationships between psychologists, psychotherapists, and divine healing practitioners also evolved. As with the beginning, the initial response of divine healing ministry practitioners towards doctors was one of hostility. Psychologists and psychotherapists faced outright rejections. Donald Gee, a British Pentecostal and editor of the *Journal of Pentecost* wrote in 1936 that psychology is not a needed help for Pentecostal people if behaviors of human mental and emotional disorders are used to displace demonic manifestations.[236] William states that Pentecostals suggested that there were evil forces working in collaboration with psychologists whose only motive is to prevent the use of God's power and

---

231. Williams, *Spirit Cure*, 56–57.
232. Williams, *Spirit Cure*, 63.
233. Williams, *Spirit Cure*, 63.
234. Williams, *Spirit Cure*, 83.
235. Strang, "Gift of Healing," 9.
236. Williams, *Spirit Cure*, 69.

obedience to His commandments. This view was shared by conservative evangelicals and fundamentalists in that time of "psychology's promotion of moral relativism."[237] William noted that Charles Price, in 1929, warned his listeners not to be involved with philosophy or psychology or any form of practice to mental helps, because man's basic problem is sin and guilt, and that can only be remedied by the activation of faith in the atonement provided by the blood of Christ.[238]

The emergence of the IHD ministry

Some Pentecostals were open to the field of psychology, even in the early days of the Pentecostal movement. These, who held a moderate view, considered psychology as a scientific knowledge giving understanding to the functions of the human mind and lesser as a healing method.[239] E. N. Bell, the Assemblies of God leader wrote: "There is no harm in psychology taught in schools and colleges if it is taught by a Christian in harmony with the Bible."[240]

Williams wrote that it was not until the midcentury (when Pentecostals began acknowledging that many ailments originated in anxiety and mental illness), that they also began accepting some of the curative processes of psychologists and psychiatrists. Demonic references still continued, albeit with greater allowance given to the role of the mind in both sickness and cure, including the naturalization of healing.[241] Oral Roberts was among the first to appreciate the development of psychology, maintaining at the same time, the importance of the deliverance ministry.[242] In the mid-1960s, Oral Roberts wrote that psychiatrists help people to understand their struggles, self-talk themselves out of their situations, and see the positives of their lives. Unlike psychiatry, Christians actually give an infusion of life instead of shifting outlooks.[243]

Gordon Lindsay acknowledged the "role of the mind in bodily sickness." In his opinion, many people in the prayer line suffered from nervous

237. Williams, *Spirit Cure*, 70.
238. Williams, *Spirit Cure*, 70.
239. Williams, *Spirit Cure*, 71.
240. Williams, *Spirit Cure*, 71.
241. Williams, *Spirit Cure*, 72.
242. Williams, *Spirit Cure*, 73.
243. Williams, *Spirit Cure*, 73.

conditions, neuroses, oppression, depression, fears and complexes and that there were oppressing spirits at work.[244] William opined that healing evangelists were 'tracking medical professionals' growing attention to the connection between the mind and body. By 1960, Donald Gee had given his approval of mind-based healing methods, affirming the validity of psychological methods to meet human needs, whilst asserting the superiority of supernatural spiritual deliverance.[245]

Meanwhile, in the 1960s, the dialogue on healing was trending towards "wholeness" instead of mere physical healing.[246] As early as 1949, Roberts quoted a doctor as saying that no real medical help can be found for those who are struggling with fears and despair that originate from their struggles with sin issues of life, and who refuse help from God. Fundamentally, a healing miracle begins from healing the inner-self.[247] Kuhlman's position was that religion is good for healing the mind, and that there is an interlocking of body, mind, and spirit.[248]

The restoration of the mind was becoming a focus for many advocating the power of right thinking and right thought to positively affect healing. In the late nineteenth century, this movement on mind restoration known as "New Thought" and popularized by Ralph Waldo Trine was gaining momentum.[249] In the Christian circle, Norman Vincent Peale in the 1950s was a big proponent of this ideology with his popular book on *The Power of Positive Thinking*.[250]

Soon, it became evident that Pentecostals were assimilating New Thought's ideology in their ministry. Oral Roberts published Peale's article "Christ's Healing Power" in his ministry magazine *Healing Waters*.[251] Gordon Lindsay's *Voice of Healing* carried Peale's article called "How Faith Shapes Events," in 1961.[252] An early influential link was that of evangelist and author E.W. Kenyon, whose healing instructions and working ideas reflected much of New Thoughts ideas on the usage of positive thinking

244. Williams, *Spirit Cure*, 75.
245. Williams, *Spirit Cure*, 75.
246. Williams, *Spirit Cure*, 87.
247. Williams, *Spirit Cure*, 87.
248. Williams, *Spirit Cure*, 87.
249. Williams, *Spirit Cure*, 76.
250. Williams, *Spirit Cure*, 77.
251. Williams, *Spirit Cure*, 77.
252. Williams, *Spirit Cure*, 77.

and encouragement and empowering words, although Kenyon denied any adoption of New Thoughts.[253] Kenyon attempted to distance himself from New Thoughts by insisting that it is not simply the power of positive thoughts and affirmation. He asserted that it is the power of Christ's death and resurrection that renders the healing power for every Christian, and that the believer on his part has to renew his mind to embrace God's will so that he can receive the benefits of the healing power of Christ.[254] Later in 1959, T.L. Osborn reproduced Kenyon's writing in his own book, with Kenyon's daughter's permission. Osborn reiterated Kenyon's position that the declaration of God's word engages Jesus Christ as the High Priest to appeal in prayer to God the Father for the release of the benefits according to God's will. He then called on Christians to declare their freedom in Christ instead of acknowledging their bondage.[255]

Kenyon's thoughts continued to influence other Pentecostals such as Chicago pastor William Durham and healing evangelist F. F. Bosworth, who were influential speakers in the first half of the twentieth century. F.F. Bosworth's work entitled *Christ the Healer* was especially influential with the teaching topic on "Our Confession," in which he gave credit to Kenyon's thoughts and writings.[256]

Meanwhile, an approach to ministering divine healing began to emerge, with Agnes Sanford as one of the early advocates of inner healing. Sanford had significant impact on Pentecostals and charismatics in this area of mental healing, inspiring many into the field of inner healing.[257] Agnes was an Episcopal laywoman whose interest in mental healing began with the illness of her third child, John. She explored New Thought and the views of mental healers like Mary Baker Eddy (she disagreed with the latter), and later embarked on her own healing ministry with writings on healing prayers.[258] She used the New Thought terminology of light, energy and vibration to explain what she understood as "God's power working in our lives."[259]

---

253. Williams, *Spirit Cure*, 78.
254. Williams, *Spirit Cure*, 78.
255. Williams, *Spirit Cure*, 80.
256. Williams, *Spirit Cure*, 80.
257. Williams, *Spirit Cure*, 100.
258. Williams, *Spirit Cure*, 100.
259. Williams, *Spirit Cure*, 100.

The Importance of IHD for Effective Discipleship

Sanford's most important contribution was her adaptation of New Thought ideas of "the power of the mind to effect healing." Williams describes how the Sanfords saw the mind as the gateway for the inflow of God's power to a person. Hence the mind was where the battle was at, and a properly guarded mind that is aligned to God allows for a free access of God's healing power to the entire being of a person. The mind that is ignorant of God is shut to God's divine power and cannot receive the benefits of God's power to give healing and life to a person.[260]

Sanford wrote that it is necessary to teach the sub-conscious mind so that godly ideas of faith, hope and life replace ideas of fear, sickness and death.[261]

This re-programming of the mind makes possible the healing of the individual's emotional and physical being.[262]

In the area of emotional healing, Sanford centers on the act of exposing and acknowledging through confession unresolved implicit memories of trauma, and then humbling oneself to receive forgiveness from God so as to have Christ's divine intervention.[263] For Sanford, these unhealed memories (referred to also as "unforgiven sins") needed to be brought to remembrance by the Holy Spirit, allowing the presence of Jesus to bring healing.[264] Sanford, referring to these unhealed memories also as "splinters in the hand", wrote that they remained hidden and continued to stir up disturbances in the person creating emotions of fear, nervousness and anxiety, but that unfortunately, we are often not aware of the causes of these disturbances.

Sanford considered this act of surrendering the unhealed memories to Jesus as "the healing exchange of an individual's sinful thought for Christ's thoughts."[265] Her explanation is that we are blocked from God's love by "thought vibrations' of our fallen and broken world. Jesus replaced our negative thought vibrations "with His thought vibrations, and received our memories and emotions of hurtful struggles with sickness, trauma and death."[266]

---

260. Williams, *Spirit Cure*, 101.
261. Williams, *Spirit Cure*, 101.
262. Williams, *Spirit Cure*, 101.
263. Williams, *Spirit Cure*, 102.
264. Williams, *Spirit Cure*, 102.
265. Williams, *Spirit Cure*, 102.
266. Williams, *Spirit Cure*, 102.

Where Might God be Placing the IHD Ministry?

Sanford used visualization to facilitate the inner healing of the emotions.[267] She wrote that the way out of our struggles is to focus on Jesus, thinking of His presence, seeing His presence with our spiritual eyes and engaging His love with our hearts.[268] For Sanford, the individual needed to take ownership of their healing through aligning their thoughts and emotions to God's continuous presence and availability to us everywhere in His creation.[269]

One major charismatic proponent who was influenced greatly by Sanford's teaching was the Roman Catholic minister Francis MacNutt.[270] Sanford's teaching made sense to MacNutt who acknowledged the findings of psychologists that in our beings, we are affected by the evils of this world that include the wounds created by others. MacNutt acknowledges that Christ came to restore and release us from all sufferings of this sort.[271] MacNutt defined inner healing as the healing that we receive from Jesus, as He heals us of the unresolved wounds of our recent and distant past that disturb us, and He in turn fills these areas of wounds with His love. He can do this because His presence is with us in the past, present and the future.[272] MacNutt's position is that the Lord does bring healing instantaneously, and that complete healing can take place.[273] He sees the limitations of counseling as that of only being able to make the counselee aware and clear about the unresolved hidden hurts of the past so that the counselee knows how to manage them, but not necessarily bringing healing.[274]

Other major proponents of inner healing include Derek Prince, Ruth Stapleton, Merlin Carothers, Rita Bennett, Dennis Bennet, Matthew Linn (charismatic Jesuit priest), David Seamands, Leanne Payne (Episcopalian healer), and Richard Dobbins (Assemblies of God minister).[275] William in reflecting upon Rita Bennett's writing, wrote that the ministry of inner healing surpasses the work of psychologists, in that healing happens

---

267. Williams, *Spirit Cure*, 102.
268. Williams, *Spirit Cure*, 102.
269. Williams, *Spirit Cure*, 102.
270. Williams, *Spirit Cure*, 103.
271. MacNutt, *Healing*, 164–65.
272. MacNutt, *Healing*, 164.
273. MacNutt, *Healing*, 169.
274. MacNutt, *Healing*, 169.
275. Williams, *Spirit Cure*, 103–7.

The Importance of IHD for Effective Discipleship

because the power of God is encountered in the ministry of inner healing, and not just involving intelligent discussions and coping strategies.[276]

Charisma magazine explains the work of inner healing as the practice of facilitating an encounter with the Holy Spirit, so that He can reveal the hidden unresolved hurts in our lives and bring them to Jesus for our healing.[277] Ruth Stapleton wrote that people receive inner healing as a result of letting Jesus enter their lives to bring peace, love and power for healing, which is not the work of any psychological therapy.[278] Stapleton displayed respect for both the disciplines of psychology and inner healing, acknowledging that "both of these positions have great truth." She believed that the integration of these two ministries for the healing of many will bring the best of both worlds of intervention together, when the Holy Spirit is given the prerogative to guide and apply the principles and findings of psychology. This will result in a greater fulfillment of God's will to bring healing to people's life, as many more ministers with greater effectiveness in inner healing, will then be raised up, to bring healing to many."[279]

One interesting observation is that later proponents of inner healing no longer used Sanford's explanation of Jesus lowering his thought-vibrations to the thought-vibrations of humanity. Instead they simply taught individuals "to imagine Jesus intervening in the painful situations of their past."[280] Visualization used by Sanford was one of the frequently used techniques by many practitioners of inner healing ministry such as Stapleton (Faith-imagination therapy), Rita Bennet, and Leanne Payne. Williams noted though that not all inner healing ministry works with imagining and seeing Jesus' intervention. Some still used prayer groups and normal counseling practices, and deliverance practices and rituals involving sacred items such as holy water in exorcism.[281]

The inner healing movement was not accepted by all Pentecostals and charismatics. In fact, various kinds of criticisms were unleashed against it. These include the views that there was a tendency to create "junior psychiatrists," to focus on the old and not the new, to blame the past for everything, navel-gazing, psycho-heresy, sin is regarded as a mistake and

276. Williams, *Spirit Cure*, 104.
277. Andrews, "What's Out of Sight," 13.
278. Stapleton, "Experience," 7–8.
279. Stapleton, "Experience," 7–8.
280. Williams, *Spirit Cure*, 105.
281. Williams, *Spirit Cure*, 106.

seeking psychological rehabilitation instead of repentance.[282] There were other objections to the inner healing movement that were related to Agnes Sanford's adoption of Freudian doctrine, Carl Jung's occult thinking, Sanford's own occult experience, and her integration of all these secular, atheistic, and occultic elements. Some equated Sanford's visualization to the occult practice of sorcery or divination used by shamans and witchdoctors. It is suggested that her views were adopted by Christian writers including Francis MacNutt, Ruth Stapleton, John and Paula Sanford, Thomas Merton, Morton Kelsey, and Richard Foster.[283] Strange it is that many Christians will readily lend themselves to secular clinical counseling which is entirely based on psychology and psychotherapy, yet denounce the involvement of God in the inner healing methodology that may or may not use the insights of psychology. The majority of seminaries and Bible colleges teach and train their graduates in clinical counseling based fully on psychology, but would not endorse the ministry of inner healing wherein God is involved in the signs and wonders of restoring the mind of the person. Finally, in John and Mark Sandford's book *Deliverance and Inner Healing,* they wrote that inner healing practitioners oftentimes deliberately disengages the philosophical ideas of psychology, whilst acknowledging the usefulness of psychological findings. [284]

Amid such criticisms and rejections however, the inner healing movement has continued to gain acceptance with Pentecostals and Charismatics alike. Quoting Williams: "Similar impulses to explicitly merge secular and spiritual forms of healing animated the ministers of inner healing who offered the faithful a form of psychotherapy not only condoned by God but also predicated on God's willingness to participate in the therapeutic process."[285]

Ruth Stapleton states that every practice, idea and life principle that is truth related touches the spiritual integrity and purity of our being. Many devoted Christians have accepted the notion that the many discoveries and ideas of psychology actually resonate with our sense of spiritual integrity although developed in worldly context. Stapleton then concluded that an experience of healing through the practice of psychology under

---

282. Williams, *Spirit Cure,* 108-11.

283. Witcombe, "The History of Christian Inner Healing," June 29, 2009, accessed July 23, 2016, https://amazingdiscoveries.org>S-deception_Sanford_Freud_Jung.

284. Sandford and Sandford, *Deliverance and Inner Healing,* 22.

285. Williams, *Spirit Cure,* 164.

The Importance of IHD for Effective Discipleship

the guidance of the Holy Spirit will lead to an emotional healing. There is an actual transformative work by the Holy Spirit of God.[286] Martin Lynch, a Catholic charismatic, commented in *Charisma* magazine, that there is a genuine Christian psychology that has been engineered by the Inner-Healing movement (a work of the Holy Spirit) that sets in place the way God has designed our human psyche versus man-made ideas of the human psyche.[287]

Amid the advances that inner healing was making, deliverance from demonic spirits continued. Derek Prince was of the conviction that the majority of Christians needed to be set free from demons that have gained control of their lives through various entrances in the person's life.[288] Prince believed that without deliverance from demons, the Christian ministry is superficial.[289] John Richards, long time Secretary to the Anglican Study Group on exorcism, stresses that exorcism must take place in the larger context of healing.[290] Peter Horrobin from Ellel Ministries, is of the conviction that a healing ministry without deliverance will "probably be less than twenty percent of what it could and should be."[291] The Sandfords wrote that they believe "deliverance and inner healing need each other. Both are incomplete and inadequate by themselves."[292] In addition, the Sandfords advocated the inclusion of a wider scheme of sanctification.[293] Neal Laranzo, a Roman Catholic Charismatic, asserts that "deliverance is an important component of Christian discipleship."[294] He does not elevate deliverance as Horrobin does, but reverts to marginalizing the deliverance component within a fairly traditional model of Christian discipleship. Loranzo believes that 98% of the work of setting free a person from evil spirits involves knowing and embracing the truth (knowing God, His truth and His work in us), refusing temptation, repenting of sin, forgiving our enemies, and negating the devil's work. He suggests that the two percent or less is also about

---

286. Stapleton, "Experience of Inner Healing," 7–8.
287. Hazard, "Inside Look," 48.
288. Collins, *Exorcism and Deliverance*, 47.
289. Prince, *They Shall Expel Demons*, 59.
290. Richards, *But Deliver Us*, 120.
291. Horrobin, *Healing through Deliverance*, 26.
292. Sandford and Sandford, *Deliverance and Inner Healing*, 25.
293. Collins, *Exorcism and Deliverance*, 99.
294. Collins, *Exorcism and Deliverance*, 195.

eviction of evil spirits. Mostly, deliverance comes as a result of praying, reading the scriptures, attending to church life and acts of communion.[295]

Although there are differences of opinions in how much is needed of deliverance from demonic spirits, there seems to be a clarion call for integrating inner healing and deliverance together and positioning the ministry of IHD as part of the act of sanctification and, therefore, of discipleship.

FROM JESUS TO NOW — WHERE IS IT GOING?

Healing was a hallmark of the ministry of Jesus, which He continually performed in the places He travelled to. Various reasons have been offered as explanations for His healing ministry (as was seen in this chapter); however, it remains consistently the case that His healings were performed with a view to restoring men and women, physically, emotionally, mentally, and spiritually. Jesus' ministry brought man back into relationship with God as Ruler, transforming man, requiring him to commit to the ways of heaven by the presence and power of the Holy Spirit.

This was how Carroll described the ministry of Jesus, mentioned earlier in this chapter. The encounter with Christ was an encounter with God, in which man experienced the work of God, specifically His power to free man from sicknesses and the works of demons. Man can then be free to submit to Christ as Lord and to the works of the Holy Spirit, aligning them with the teachings of Christ and transforming them into the image of Christ.

In the first three hundred years, the church continued the work of Christ in miracles of healing and deliverance from demonic spirits. Yet by man's own decision, it was decided that God was no longer performing any miracles and healings after the passing of the last apostle. Paul, in his first letter to Timothy warned against allowing worldly and empty chatter, and the opposing arguments of what is falsely called "knowledge, which some have professed and thus gone astray from the faith" (1 Tim 6:20-21), to flourish. Yet, the church adopted the philosophy of Aristotle as its basis for defining the relationship between God and man, including his ideas of cessationism and dispensation. In so doing, the church leadership negated the validity of God's power and the works of God through Christ in miracles, divine healings, and deliverance. Christianity was reduced to a set of doctrines, behaviors, and missions directed by human reasoning as the prime

---

295. Loranzo, *Unbound*, 195.

The Importance of IHD for Effective Discipleship

motivator, subtly and significantly reducing the experiential relationship and work of the Holy Spirit.

However, God was not to be negated by man's ingenuity and reason—He continued to perform His miracles of healing with those who would allow Him to, creating revivals such as the Holiness Movement, Faith Cure Movement, and the Pentecostal Movement. The development of Christianity in Korea is an example of Christian leadership that chose to follow the biblical ministry of Jesus in healing and deliverance, as opposed to the doctrine of cessationism. While it was the Presbyterian missionaries (who held to the doctrine of cessationism) who originally brought the gospel into Korea, the Koreans quickly took over the work of the gospel, choosing instead to follow the biblical model of Jesus' ministry. Hence, divine healing was a major feature of Protestantism and a tool for conversion there.[296]

This is also true with the Christians in China who read the Bible literally and prescriptively witnessing the acts of God in divine healing.[297] God is in the act of restoring man through His miraculous acts of healing, so that man can be freed from the works of the enemy and be transformed by Him into the image of Christ. It was the apostle Paul who said in Phil 1:6 that "For I am confident of this very thing, that He who began a good work in you will perfect it until the day of Christ Jesus." In other words, God is at work personally and directly, and He will continue to do it. From the tracings of history, God would not be stopped!

From the time of the early church, divine healing was focused in the area of the physical healing of the body and deliverance from demonic spirits, although the ministry of Jesus saw the healing of the body, mind, and emotions of the person. Eventually, in the twentieth century, divine healing began focusing on the restoration of the mind and emotions of the person, resulting in what is now known as the inner healing movement. Some of today's major ministries of inner healing include Ellel Ministries, Elijah House Ministries, Cleansing Stream Ministries, Restoring the Foundations Ministries, Ancient Path Ministries, Sozo Ministries, Theophostic Ministries, DEW Ministries, and many others.

However, for a long time, these ministries were seen only as "hospital ministry" where the sick go to receive help, and not as an integral part of the discipleship structure of the church. As an example of this, I remember an incident that speaks rather loudly of such a perception. Two young men

---

296. Kim, "Reenchanted: Divine Healing," 268–69.
297. Oblau, "Divine Healing," 320-21.

were standing outside my office door, which had the DEW sign on it. One young man asked the other, "What is this DEW ministry about?" The other replied, "This is for those persons with real serious trouble."

Few have understood DEW as a preventive and discipling ministry: preventive as in bringing healing into people's emotional hurts so that they do not continue to deteriorate to a worse state; and discipling, in that its teaching helps people understand how they should be growing in the Lord—where they need the Lord to help them make corrections to their lives through confession, repentance, forgiveness, and renunciation, and then to encounter the Lord Himself for transformation.

As a movement, the healing ministry has had to battle its way through periods of rejection and fighting its way up the hill of acknowledgement and acceptance that this is truly God's provision for the restoration and transformation of man into the image of Christ. It is time to consider bringing the IHD ministry that Jesus did so frequently, back into the discipleship structure of the local church. In the next chapter, I will explore the relevance of this ministry for this current season of time in church history.

5

Discipleship that Includes IHD for the Post-Modern Era

JAMES HOUSTON DEFINED DISCIPLESHIP as simply "learning how to follow Christ."[1] Chris Shirley refers to discipleship as "the process of following Jesus." She says that it is the mission of the local church to partner with God to extend the gospel all over the world through the work of making disciples (Matt 28:18-20). In her description, every church should be made up of believers who are giving themselves to the task of discipling other believers. This is an ongoing learning journey of "following me as I follow Christ"—the main subject of Christ-centered education.[2] She further elaborates that the church in Acts 2:42-47, undertook the task of helping people with life challenges to become disciples through teaching, building relationships and through worshipping God.[3] Shirley then suggests that the acts of discipleship described in these scriptures give an idea of the activities that are necessary after baptism. Some key acts of discipleship include soul-winning, teaching, building relationships, celebration, and works of touching lives for change.[4] Discipleship in the local church is an intentional systematic program towards the spiritual formation of the person to be like Christ in their being and doing.

1. Houston, "Future of Spiritual Formation," 131.
2. Shirley, "It Takes a Church," 210.
3. Shirley, "It Takes a Church," 212.
4. Shirley, "It Takes a Church," 212.

Discipleship that Includes IHD for the Post-Modern Era

There remains an inadequacy in the current discipleship structural process. There is a further need for the inclusion of an IHD-ministry, to enable discipleship in the local church to come into a fuller partnership with the Holy Spirit, in His work of forming Christ in the believer. The desired result is a discipleship process that will be closer to the discipleship ministry of Jesus and the early church, a greater transformational discipleship process towards a healthier Christian maturity, with an experiential existential God-encounter, relevant to post-modernistic demands.

DISCIPLESHIP WEAKNESS EXPOSED IN THE POST-MODERN ERA

The demands of the post-modernistic generation reflect a paradigm shift of values and attitudes that influence the receptivity of religious belief. Heath White says that post-modernism is a perspective of how life should be viewed, shared by a generation of people who have become young adults.[5]

Postmodernism evolved out of modernism, which in turn, evolved out of pre-modernism, after the age of Enlightenment.[6] Postmodernism rejects authority and reasoning. White describes Postmoderns as those who no longer trust in established leadership and logic, and are at a loss as to what makes sense.

Postmodernism takes the position that "the big questions in life have no definitive answers".[7] The post-modernistic generation tends towards relativism, constructivism, and pragmatism.[8] White defines post-modernistic generation relativism as "the idea that truth varies from person to person (radical relativism), or from society to society (cultural relativism)."[9] Constructivism describes truths as being constructed by different individuals and societies and it is not a common truth that is discovered.[10] Hence, you are entitled to your own truth as constructed by yourself or your society. Pragmatism says that whatever works for a person is truth for that person. Hence it is all about what you intend to achieve in life, and so one truth is

---

5. White, *Post Modernism 101*, 11.
6. White, *Post Modernism 101*, 23.
7. White, *Post Modernism 101*, 48.
8. White, *Post Modernism 101*, 49.
9. White, *Post Modernism 101*, 49.
10. White, *Post Modernism 101*, 49.

The Importance of IHD for Effective Discipleship

different from one person to another or from one culture to another, each defining truth according to what each wants to achieve.[11]

Susanne Johnson described this generation as having many varied groups with an intolerance for traditional religious institutions, a distrust of organization, and a sense of dishonor towards governmental bodies.[12] In addition, she says Postmoderns have a greater attraction to an experience-based, highly involved and evaluative mode of education over lectures and the one-way teacher-to-student style of learning. Their interest is in the free interpretation of learners instead of content teaching, and they do not gravitate towards religious establishments and doctrines..[13] The significance of this shift is a search for spirituality that is experiential and not just an intellectual cognitive assimilation of doctrinal propositions, and the practice of doing good. Herein lies the serious gap between current discipleship processes practiced in local churches that tend towards orthodoxis and orthopraxis, and what is actually needed for discipleship to be relevant and effective to the post-modernistic generation. Orthodoxis approaches religion as a matter of the head (promoting right beliefs), and orthopraxis sees religion as a matter of the hands (doing the right things). Both are no longer sufficient for the post-modernistic generation of discipleship towards the spiritual formation of the person of Christ in the believer.[14]

Typically, the current discipleship process involves the activities listed by Matthew Meyer, which are, becoming an active member of a Christian community of faith; prayer; studying the Bible; reading good books and magazines; disciplining yourself for regular devotional times; the use of music; journal writing; paying attention to dreams; recognizing, developing, and using personal gifts; sharing your faith with others; fasting; choosing a spiritual friend; expressing your faith through service; trying a mantra, or meaningful ritual.[15] The inadequacy of the current discipleship approaches has always been there but it is now brought into prominent exposure because of the demands of the post-modernistic generation. What the post-modernistic generation is looking for is a Christian spiritual

---

11. White, *Post Modernism 101*, 49.
12. Johnson, "Christian Spiritual Formation," 301.
13. Johnson, "Christian Spiritual Formation," 310.
14. Johnson, "Christian Spiritual Formation," 312.
15. Meyer, "Practical Dimensions," 106.

formation in discipleship, which emphasizes religion as a matter of the heart and real to life experience, an orthokardia approach.[16]

What is currently at stake in Christian discipleship is the genuine experience of God that transforms the inner self—the spiritual experience of being touched by God and being in touch with God. This is what is needed to make discipleship relevant and effective for the present generation of believers and pre-believers. Unfortunately, Johnson rightly says that Christianity is perceived as a collection of statements of assertions that gives details of a Christian's beliefs and known historical facts. These assertions include established ideas of beliefs, practices and signs that explain their ontological ideology of existence—to be a Christian is to know and embrace this Christian ideology. [17]

Through the years, church history has shown how discipleship has evolved from a dynamic relational experience with God and involvement with God as in *Christi partipatio,* to that of *Christi imitation,* which is about living an ethical life that reflects the life that Christ lived. This is no longer enough for Christian formation to an experiential existential demand for a real encounter with God. The orthodoxis and orthopraxis approaches to discipleship that have been a longstanding practice of Christian discipleship are inadequate for Christian discipleship today. The orthodoxis model over-emphasizes rigid adherences to established ideas of doctrine excessively to the point that believers stay away and dissociate themselves from any form of personal spiritual encounters with God.[18] The orthopraxis model in turn, is charged with failing to adequately help people experience the reality of God's infinite greatness and power, so much so that they hold firmly to their experiential knowledge of God's reality.[19] Johnson says that orthokardia meets the needs of this generation's demand for real and genuine experiential encounters with God that touch their inner beings.[20] It's the experiential existential encounter with God that results in the formation of inner-self and inner-being that is being sought after by believers. For Christian discipleship to be wholesome, there must be the inclusion of orthokardia to the orthodoxis and orthopraxis that already exist. Kierkegaard expressed that Christians who have only head knowledge of Christianity

---

16. Johnson, "Christian Spiritual Formation," 312.
17. Johnson, "Christian Spiritual Formation," 315.
18. Johnson, "Christian Spiritual Formation," 313.
19. Johnson, "Christian Spiritual Formation," 313.
20. Johnson, "Christian Spiritual Formation," 312.

The Importance of IHD for Effective Discipleship

are only Christians by behavior and are as good as unbelievers.[21] Christianity to him is not behavioral but an inner being with experiential reality of their belief in God[22]

For discipleship to be orthokardia in its approach, focus has to be given to real experiences of the presence, the work, and the power of the Holy Spirit, in and through the lives of the believer. Interestingly, Oliver Davis suggested that the reason that most Christian youths decide to jettison Jesus after high school, is because they never knew the God who is present in the person of the Holy Spirit.[23] Essentially, there was no real experience of the presence, relationship, work, and power of the Holy Spirit. Davis says that "the *ethos* in our churches in the West has largely disregarded the Spiritual presence of God."[24] In other words, the Holy Spirit does not get a lot of attention, and is not seen as the means to a vital connective experiential relationship with Jesus, in which Jesus becomes the formative Leader-Teacher and the believer as the receptive follower-pupil.[25] Davis suggests that the role of the Holy Spirit must be seen in the economy of salvation as that of converting and completing the work of salvation in the person, and making the ministry of Jesus Christ clearly manifested and experienced amongst believers.[26] He adds that discipleship is about the Holy Spirit's work of customizing the revelation of God's intended truth to each believer, bringing about a bonding between the believer and his Lord.[27]

The Holy Spirit must be acknowledged as the third Person in the Trinity of God who is sovereign, missional, immanent, and relational.[28] In His sovereignty, He acts according to His own divine logic and will for all of our good.[29] The Holy Spirit is missional in His involvement in the ongoing mission of God in the work of reconciliation and redemption. In this missional role, He draws us into partnership with Him, calling us to be disciples of Jesus, empowered by Him to establish the kingdom of God in

---

21. Johnson, "Christian Spiritual Formation," 317.
22. Johnson, "Christian Spiritual Formation," 317.
23. Johnson, "Christian Spiritual Formation," 324.
24. Davis, "Transformation Theology," 328.
25. Davis, "Transformation Theology," 328.
26. Davis, "Transformation Theology," 326.
27. Davis, "Transformation Theology," 326.
28. Davis, "Transformation Theology," 331–35.
29. Davis, "Transformation Theology," 330.

Discipleship that Includes IHD for the Post-Modern Era

the mission of God.[30] God, the Holy Spirit, is immanent in that though He is ontologically distinct from creation, He chooses to be present and is continuously involved in our existence, intervening and participating persistently and decisively to bring about the fulfillment of His will for us.[31] God the Holy Spirit is relational in that God created us for relationship both with Him and with each other.

Davis says that the sin that blocks our communion with God is overcome in Christ, and God recovers His intended relationship with man at Creation through the Holy Spirit.[32] It is about partnering with the Holy Spirit in an experiential relationship, with us yielding to His work of transformation as we follow Him that makes us disciples of Jesus. The local church effort at discipleship should facilitate all of the transformational relational work that the Holy Spirit wants to do, in and through the life of the believer, for the good of all—the believer and the pre-believer. Davis says that to create a spirit-filled discipleship for young adults, the church needs to accept her responsibility to be a parenting body of the Holy Spirit for believers. To be a spiritual parenting body, there must be a spiritual revelation amongst believers that opens the access to their relationship with God the Holy Spirit, who is "sovereign, missional, immanent and relational." Otherwise, believers will eventually conclude that God has undefined intentions, relates only according to usefulness and performance, transcendent and without power for real encounters.[33]

To have a church as a "nursery of the Holy Spirit," the church discipleship structural process must embrace the ministry of the Holy Spirit in the church through the miraculous spiritual gifts. The ministry of the Holy Spirit embraces the basic purpose of Christ appearing, which is to destroy the works of the devil (1 John 3:8).[34] Peter described Jesus' mission on earth in Acts 10:38 as being anointed by God with the power of the Holy Spirit, and demonstrated the presence of God with Him, as He went around with all kinds of acts of kindness and goodness, healing and setting free many who were oppressed by the devil. The Gospels testify to the many activities of Jesus in acts of healing and deliverance forming forty-four percent of Matthew, sixty-five percent of Mark, twenty-nine percent

---

30. Davis, "Transformation Theology," 332.
31. Davis, "Transformation Theology," 332–33.
32. Davis, "Transformation Theology," 335.
33. Davis, "Transformation Theology," 336.
34. Ruthven, "Imitation," 71.

The Importance of IHD for Effective Discipleship

of Luke and thirty percent of John.[35] Ruthven says that signs and wonders must be considered as a very important part of following Christ, if New Testament discipleship is understood to be about reproducing the life of the discipler.[36] For Ruthven, the significance of a subject matter is clearly seen in the proportion of content written on the subject matter. The numerous records of healing and deliverance from evil are indicative of the high importance of the supernatural spiritual gifts of the Holy Spirit.[37] In addition, Paul names a variety of the manifestations of the Holy Spirit that are meant for the common good—the word of wisdom; the word of knowledge; faith; healing; miracles; prophecy; distinguishing spirits; kinds of tongues; and interpretation of tongues (1 Cor 12:4–10, 28). All of these ministry gifts of the Holy Spirit are the powerful experiential encounters with the works of God's love for the building up of the believers.

The Psalmist in Ps 103:1–5 says:

> Bless the Lord, O my soul, and all that is within me, bless His holy name. Bless the Lord, O my soul, and forget none of His benefits; Who pardons all your iniquities, Who heals all your diseases; Who redeems your life from the pit, Who crowns you with love and compassion; Who satisfies your years with good things, so that your youth is renewed like the eagle.

The restoration of wholeness to the life of the believer is at the heart of God and therefore should be provided for in the structural processes of discipleship in the local church. This also touches the core of our human self with the love of God, and the God-encounter element becomes pertinent for the believer, much more so for the generation of the post-modernistic era. In the survey of the responses of 843 people at the DEW ministry weekend, eighty-nine percent of the participants indicated in their testimony forms that they had a personal encounter with God; and eighty-seven percent experienced the removal of hindrances to their spiritual growth. This is an aspect of orthokardia that is evident through the ministry of inner healing and deliverance. Jack Hayford, Chancellor of the King's College and Seminary wrote that Jesus' plan for His church is not simply about the church receiving the benefits that the Cross provides (such as evicting demons, healing and all of the operations of the supernatural gifts), but also the call for those who come to Him to disciple others, just as they themselves have

---

35. Ruthven, "Imitation," 72.
36. Ruthven, "Imitation," 72.
37. Ruthven, "Imitation," 72.

Discipleship that Includes IHD for the Post-Modern Era

been discipled. Hayford says that discipling people to grow in Christ is a definite priority of discipleship, and that this must include setting people free from bondages, and must also include healing, for them to embrace the full blessings God intends.[38]

Hayford endorses the deliverance ministry as a central part of Christian discipleship.[39]

TACT'S GUIDELINE FOR DISCIPLESHIP STRUCTURE (IHD INCLUSIVE) DESIGN

TACT (Theological and Cultural Thinkers) has laid out a good set of propositional statements for developing a structural discipleship framework (which is inclusive of IHD) in the local church. Formed in September 2002, TACT is made up of theologians, cultural thinkers, and spiritual-formation practitioners.[40] It was formed to help churches become "spiritual formation" churches.[41] In a book titled *The Kingdom of Life*, seven process elements and three theological elements of spiritual formation are given to guide churches in designing a discipleship process for spiritual formation.[42]

	Process Elements
Element 1	The good news of God is that God is at work to form us into the image of Christ when we choose to submit our lives to the Lordship of Christ. The work of God is full of His goodness to create the beauty of God's kingdom, which happens only according to our response to align with the will of God.
Element 2	Spiritual formation is the outcome of an intimate communion with God and with each other. Our identity is realized and formed, as a body of believers extend favor to us and relentlessly believes in us, enabling us to live "in trust, love, grace, humility, dignity and justice." This empowers us (the body of believers) to help each other to discover and embrace God's truth and also to give the truth to unbelievers.
Element 3	Spiritual formation is about being formed in the image of Christ as His disciples. It demands a diligent and deliberate attention to allow ourselves to be transformed to be like Christ in our private and community life, as we learn to live our lives according to His instructions.

38. Hayward, *God's Cleansing Stream*, 12.
39. Hayward, *God's Cleansing Stream*, 12.
40. Andrews, *Kingdom of Life*, 10.
41. Andrews, *Kingdom of Life*, 10.
42. Andrews, *Kingdom of Life*, 18.

Process Elements	
Element 4	Spiritual formation to becoming like Christ takes a lifetime transformational work that begins with the formation of our being, not just a work of behavioral change.
Element 5	Spiritual formation as a lifetime transformational work involves the work of God in bringing healing to our brokenness, hurts and our rebelliousness. It is a change that results from an encounter with God's power and not human therapeutic interventions.
Element 6	Spiritual formation happens when God intervenes in our moments of "woundedness" (experienced because we live in this fallen world), and turns those moments of our suffering into moments of opportunity for His good work in our lives, so that we are strengthened to fulfill His purposes for our lives. The end result of our encounters with His love in our suffering is a love and compassion in us to bless this suffering world.
Element 7	Spiritual formation into the likeness of Christ nurtures in us a heart after God's heart, giving us a passion and heart to partner with God in His mission to bring people into a reconciled relationship with Him. In addition, as we embrace the heart of God, we pursue justice, love and mercy to remove sinful established structures and expressions in our cultures and our society. This becomes a key concern for us as believers.
Theological Elements	
Element 8	"The theology of spiritual formation emerges from the Trinitarian nature of God—relational, loving, gracious, mutually submissive, and unified in will."
Element 9	Spiritual formation is the Holy Spirit's work in our lives to give us a capacity to relate and respond to God and to transform us into the likeness of Christ. It is the Holy Spirit in us that gives guidance and gifts, motivation and power, to live holy and exemplary lives amongst the body of believers and in the world.
Element 10	Spiritual formation is the result of adhering to God's Word as the absolute authority for living life, providing us with revelational truths that define an understanding of godly spirituality and its practices, that are acceptable to God.

Table 1: 10 Elements for Spiritual Formation[43]
(Summary of TRACT's 10 elements of spiritual formation)

These ten elements are good wholesome guiding principles to developing a discipleship structural process that is inclusive of the orthodoxis, orthopraxis, and orthokardia approaches to discipleship. The elements are

43. Andrews, *Kingdom of Life*, 18–23.

Discipleship that Includes IHD for the Post-Modern Era

anchored theologically (Elements 8–10) on the Trinitarian God, with a reliance on the relationship and work of the Holy Spirit, and with the Bible as its source content. It relates to God, acknowledging Him as sovereign (Elements 1 and 8), missional (Elements 7 and 9), immanent (Elements 5, 6, and 9) and relational (Elements 2, 3, 8, and 9). Orthokardia is provided for in Elements 2, 4, 5, 6, 8 and 9 because there is a strong focus on encountering God experientially, leading to a transformational change of the inner self to being more like Christ. The place of inner healing and deliverance in the discipleship structural process is being provided for in Element 5, which has to do with the work of God in bringing healing to our brokenness, hurts and our rebelliousness.

Keith Meyer addresses the necessity of Element 5. He says that a change in the believer's life involves changes that is not just a result of living a Christian life, but a change in the being of the person involving all of his thinking, physical body, emotions, will, spirit and relationships.[44]

He talks about how many believers are doing what Dallas Willard calls "sin management"—managing sin from happening again instead of repentance and real change, or mortification of these sins.[45] Meyer affirms that all church programs and activities are means that we use at attempting to change lives, but yet many lives remain the same with no real change in their being.[46] He cites Willow Creek Community Church's conclusion on the analysis of her own discipleship program. The conclusion is that the programs and activities have failed to create transformed lives other than a conversion experience, and that courses in spiritual disciplines were not sufficient to create change.[47]

Meyer says that without helping the woundedness in a believer's life, anything we do is merely double dressing the person with another set of behaviors to manage sin, but not a change of heart and life.[48] He adds that there needs to be a healing of the woundedness and issues of sin and rebelliousness in an environment of compassion, mercy and grace. Without this healing, all activities of spiritual disciplines and learning end up being a performance key indicator of spiritual maturity, an achievement people are driven to perform, and a faulty indicator of maturity, resulting in no

---

44. Andrews, *The Kingdom of Life*, 146.
45. Andrews, *The Kingdom of Life*, 147.
46. Andrews, *The Kingdom of Life*, 147.
47. Andrews, *The Kingdom of Life*, 150.
48. Andrews, *The Kingdom of Life*, 150.

The Importance of IHD for Effective Discipleship

real change into the likeness of Christ.[49] It is the partnering with God to treat the "spiritual me" or the "spiritual self"—"the true, the intimate, the ultimate, the permanent me"—described as the "core" and "sanctuary" of our life, that makes the real difference for continued growth in our identity in Christ.[50]

VARIOUS IHD-MINISTRIES THAT CAN BE ADOPTED

There are already many inner healing and deliverance ministries that can help local churches build a similar ministry to bring healing to the woundedness and bondage of believers, within the discipleship structural process of the local church. Some of these include The Cleansing Stream, Ellel Ministries, Elijah House Ministries, Restoring the Foundations Ministries, Restorative Gateways Ministries, RAM Ministries, Ancient Pathway Ministries, SOZO, Wholeness Through Christ Ministry, and DEW Ministry.

Cleansing Stream provides "programs which are conducted in the local churches led by and under the covering of pastoral leadership."[51] There are four seminars.[52] The Basic Seminar is a, 8–12 week series of classes preparing participants to receive healing and deliverance, culminating in a one day retreat. After the Basic Seminar is the Advanced-Cleansing Stream Discipleship, which trains participants to minister deliverance on a team in the local church, during Cleansing Stream events. There are also the Cleansing Stream Youth (tailored to meet the needs of youths), and the Marriage Live (designed to help married couples).

Elijah House International's mission is "to train believers to bring healing and transformation to the inner man through biblically-based revelations."[53] Their basic program comprises of three levels of training.[54] Elijah House 100-level Seminar Series for Groups is designed for use by pastors and small group leaders to use in home studies or small groups. Elijah House School of Ministry—Training Course 201 teaches "foundational principles and tools for dealing with common issues to trace bad

---

49. Andrews, *The Kingdom of Life*, 152.
50. Poll and Smith, "Spiritual Self," 130.
51. Cleansing Stream, "About Us."
52. Cleansing Stream, "About Us."
53. Elijah House, "Elijah House Training," para. 2.
54. Elijah House, "Elijah House Training," para. 2.

Discipleship that Includes IHD for the Post-Modern Era

fruits to bitter roots formed in the heart", and to release these from the believer through prayer. Elijah House School of Ministry—Training Course 202 equips the believer to apply 201-level skills to specific problems such as sexual issues, shame, depression, generational sins, and others. Elijah House Advanced 300-level Training is an internship program to further develop the ministry skills and understanding of the participants.

Ellel Ministries defined its work as that of helping people to receive their healing from God, to build and intimate relationship with God, to know God better and to fulfill God's plans for their lives. They do this in two ways. Firstly, they bring the prayer ministry to people so that they can receive healing that frees them to grow in a deeper relationship with. Secondly, they conduct training events to believers to help other receive healing and equip others. Training events include many short courses (1–3 days), covering different aspects of the healing ministry; specialist training schools (7–12 days), and longer training schools of up to 40 weeks.[55]

Restoring the Foundations centers their teaching on four core revelations. These are Generational Sins and Curses, Ungodly Beliefs, Life's Hurts and Demonic Oppression, which are seen as four sources to human problems. Their training investigates the troubles created by each of these areas, and provides understanding and skills "to identify the unique combination of each source and its contribution to the problems in the hearts and lives of those receiving ministry."[56] They also provide specialty seminars that include Marriage and Pre-Marriage; How to be Free from the Shame-Fear-Control Stronghold; Sexuality; and Overcoming Rejections.[57]

I am not qualified to provide any critique of the strengths and weaknesses of these ministries as I am not involved sufficiently with them nor trained by them. However, I can provide some general comments. Some IHD-ministries have positioned themselves strictly to train pastors and church workers to do the ministry. Righteous Act Ministries (RAM), Restoration Gateways Ministries (which specializes in Dissociation Identity Disorders and Satanic Ritual Abuse), SOZO, and Restoring the Foundations, are some such ministries. While they are effective at providing training for building up an IHD-team, one is more likely however to end up with a "hospital unit" or an ad hoc "medical team", that is present to minister to those who are seriously emotionally wounded or spiritually oppressed.

---

55. Ellel Ministries, accessed 23rd July 2019. https://ellel.org/sg/about/faq.
56. Restoring the Foundations, "Our Building Blocks," para. 3.
57. Restoring the Foundations, "Seminars & Events," para. 3.

The Importance of IHD for Effective Discipleship

Others have formal teaching programs that are focused on helping believers understand the hindrances to their spiritual growth. Ministries such as Ellel Ministries, Elijah House Ministries, Cleansing Stream, and DEW Ministries are examples of such ministries, with a program of teaching and prayer-counseling designed as a discipleship strategy to fit the local church discipleship structural processes. The emphasis of their teaching differs significantly. Some emphasize mostly on exposing the hindrances and on understanding how to receive ministry. For example, the teaching may expose what sexual sins are, and the struggles with sexual sins, but may not teach sufficiently on Godly sexuality and relationships. Others (like Ellel Ministries and DEW Ministries), would have a better balance of exposing the hindrances and teachings on how to live a healthy Christian life. There is a need for a balance in the teaching, so that a person sees the need for correction in his life, and learns how to now live his life correctly, according to Biblical principles and truths.

Some IHD-ministries provide ministry on a mass level, like at a weekend encounter. Some participants will receive much and some will not. The danger is that this latter group may leave thinking that they have dealt with their issues simply because they have prayed, when, in fact, no real healing and deliverance has actually taken place.

Being able to receive ministry individually—i.e. being ministered to personally and directly by a ministry worker—is always preferred so that issues can be properly identified. It needs to be acknowledged however that how far the healing goes, depends on the honesty of the participants, and their "ripeness" or readiness to receive ministry. In addition, one-to-one ministry provides for better follow-up in the discipleship process, and referrals for help can be more properly and more efficiently done. Further, referrals can include pastoral care, mentoring, accountability, counseling and psychiatric help. These are some important considerations when picking an IHD-ministry to fit the existing discipleship structure of a church.

There are many more ministries that can be invited to bring the healing dimension into the discipleship structure of the local church. The church leadership needs though, to decide on the format and form that best fit their vision of what the ministry should be for them. Adopting IHD as an integral part of its discipleship structure would mean that everyone in the church is encouraged to attend the IHD-ministry, so that they can be freed from the hindrances that impede their growth into Christlikeness.

Discipleship that Includes IHD for the Post-Modern Era

IHD AS AN INTEGRAL COMPONENT OF DISCIPLESHIP, NOT A HOSPITAL UNIT

Bringing in one of these ministries into the local church ministry structure will add TACT Element 5 into the discipleship structure of the church. However, there is one major problem that actually hinders the full potential of the IHD-ministry from becoming a fully beneficial arm of a structural process of discipleship that every believer can benefit from. IHD has been mostly carried out by para-church organizations. Hence, the ministry has always been outside the structure and spiritual covering of the local church, and not seen as part of the discipleship structure. Participants are commonly made up of those who face some form of emotional or spiritual challenges. As such, it is inevitable that IHD ministries have often been seen as "hospital units." Functionally, the primary purpose of the IHD-ministry has been recognised as a ministry body to bring healing to the believer. If this is all that it is acknowledged for however, it will only exist to bring healing to those who are seriously broken, wounded and spiritually oppressed. It will therefore remain as a "hospital unit" or a "medical team."

This paradigm of IHD as a "hospital unit" needs to change. Seen differently, IHD-ministry can become a very essential link to rebuilding foundations of believers for effective discipleship growth. Much of IHD-ministry identifies with the four core areas that Restoring the Foundations Ministries addresses, when ministering to a believer. These four core areas are "Sins of the Fathers and Resulting Curses," "Ungodly Beliefs," "Soul/Spirit Hurts," and "Demonic Oppression."[58] The "Sins of the Fathers and Resulting Curses" has to do with what we have inherited from our parents and ancestors that now hinders our walk with God.[59] This involves our participation in their sinful ways and the consequences of their sins that we continue to live in. Ministering into this area has to do with identifying and removing these areas of ungodly participation, and embracing our inheritance in Christ.

The ministry into the area of "Ungodly Beliefs" has to do with removing the half-truths and untruths in the believer's mind that were formed from the hurtful events of his past.[60] These can form strongholds in our minds which set us against the knowledge of God (2 Cor 10:4–5). Ungodly

---

58. Kylstra and Kylstra, *Integrated Approach*, 15–17.
59. Kylstra and Kylstra, *Integrated Approach*, 59–106.
60. Kylstra and Kylstra, *Integrated Approach*, 107–49.

The Importance of IHD for Effective Discipleship

beliefs need to be identified and removed and replaced with godly beliefs (Rom 12:2).

"Soul/Spirit Hurts" are areas of hurts that we have experienced in our lives' journey, which need to be properly taken care of through forgiveness, and through letting God heal the emotional wounds.[61] Rejection is one of the most undiagnosed and untreated hurts of many believers. Many times, we manifest this rejection in sinful behaviors that keep tripping us up, in our walk with Christ. Healing our sexual identity and hurts is also a part of this area of ministry. Ministering into the areas of demonic oppression has to do with removing the foothold of the enemy in our lives.[62]

When we deal with all these four areas in the believer's life, we are enabling the person to allow God to break the ungodly foundations of his life and rebuild God's foundation for living as a disciple of Jesus Christ. This is about tearing down ungodly foundations and building in God's foundation. It involves educating the believer on what is right and wrong according to the Word of God, and partnering with the Holy Spirit to remove the wrong and set in the right. This rebuilding of foundation gives liberty to the believer to pursue God and to grow into maturity in Christ, as God transforms him in the journey of sanctification.

Every believer struggles with these four areas, albeit some to a larger extent than others. If every believer is given an opportunity to let the Holy Spirit rebuild his foundations, discipleship would be even more effectively achieved. In addition, believers will encounter the love of God in a very personal way as the Holy Spirit ministers to them. They may then experience orthokardia, as has been the experience of many. This is discipleship that is cognitive, healing, liberating, transformational, and experiencing God.

The IHD-ministry is better and more effectively employed for transformational work, when it is not tailored just to bring healing to the seriously wounded and oppressed. Instead, IHD-ministry should be made available to all, so that everyone can unload their ungodly baggage of the past and experience healing, rebuilding of foundations and transformation that will release them to pursue God. In addition, it is preventive in that it allows the believer to encounter God to release them from the baggage of the past, and to receive from God as 2 Tim 1:7 says: "God has not given you a spirit of fear but of love, power, and a sound mind" (NIV). Hence, it

---

61. Kylstra and Kylstra, *Integrated Approach*, 150–98.
62. Kylstra and Kylstra, *Integrated Approach*, 200–68.

Discipleship that Includes IHD for the Post-Modern Era

will help prevent the believer from reaching breaking point mentally as he faces the challenges in life. It is much better to have them grow healthily, than struggling silently, till they have a breakdown mentally, and then the recovery will be very difficult.

As mentioned earlier, most churches do already have some form of discipleship structure in place. If one takes on TACT's suggestion as a guideline, one would simply include or add on an IHD-ministry into the whole discipleship structure of the church. This does improve the discipleship structure overall, because there is at least a place for people to go to, so that they can resolve the deeper issues of their lives. However, it will become a "hospital unit" for the seriously emotionally hurting and spiritually oppressed. What I am advocating is not a "hospital unit" or a "medical team" that is activated when needed on an ad hoc basis. Rather, I am advocating that the IHD-ministry comes under the local church covering as a ministry, and as a discipleship strategy for all to attend.

6

Conclusion

An IHD Ministry that is Fully Integrated in a Church Discipleship Structure

THE PRIMARY PURPOSE OF the IHD ministry is bringing a person to wholeness-in-Christ through healing of the mind and emotions, and deliverance from demonic oppression. I have defined wholeness-in-Christ in Chapter 1 to mean a believer who has experienced emotional/spiritual healing, who has been released from demonic bondages and footholds if any, who has renewed his mind to align with God's truth, who has encountered God's love, and who now identifies himself as a child of God loved by God, no longer bound by sinful behaviors of the past, but reconciled in his relationship with others to love them, and is submitted to be discipled towards further growth in Christ, to live according to the will of God and in pursuit of serving God's destiny for his life.

Tracing biblical and church history, it can be observed that IHD was a frequent and impactful ministry of Jesus in restoring a person from mental and emotional turmoil to a sound mind, so that they may discover and grow in their relationship with Jesus, God the Father, and the community. In Mark 16:15–18, Jesus commanded His disciples to preach the Gospel. He promised that they would carry on the ministry that He first established—working deliverance with signs and wonders following, to all in need. The first 300 years of church history contains records of Christians continuing the work of Christ with healings, deliverance and evidence of signs and wonders. However, the church had, after that, chosen to follow the philosophy of Aristotle, which resulted in a declaration of the cessation of the work of God in healing, deliverance and all works related to signs and wonders. God, however, continued His movement of healing and deliverance outside of the local church governance and authority. Eventually, with the arrival of the Pentecostal movement, healing and deliverance became a ministry again seen in the churches. However, it would be much later before the inner healing movement was birthed outside of the local church and carried by para-church organizations. Its primary concentration was to bring mental and emotional healing, as well as to release believers from spiritual oppression.

Theologically, IHD as a ministry, is part of man's response in the act of discipleship to God's work of sanctification through the work of the Holy Spirit. Sanctification is instantaneous and also progressive. Discipleship and IHD is the response of believers to God's progressive work of sanctification to create in us the likeness of Christ. This clearly was the instruction of Christ to His disciples to be involved in God's progressive work of sanctification, most aptly expressed by Jesus washing His disciples' feet. He underlined the importance that His disciples should continue in their "being conformed to the image of Christ". As such, the ministry of the disciple in the act of discipleship must bear the ontological realities of the praxis of Christ, through the work and power of the Holy Spirit. IHD needs to be an essential work of discipleship that touches the life of all believers because everyone, to a greater or a lesser extent, has suffered from the fallen nature of humankind through their respective life journeys before knowing Jesus as Savior and Lord. This work, of realigning the mind, healing of the emotions, and deliverance from any demonic spiritual footholds, brings wholeness to a person, freeing him to respond to discipleship in the pursuit of God's will.

In addition, the IHD ministry is a relevant existential experience of the ontological realities of Christ's presence and work by the Holy Spirit, for a post-modernistic generation of pre-believers and believers. Its orthokardia (right-heartedness) experience makes for pragmatic and constructive discipleship that is personal, immediate, personally benefitting, and opens them to a real God-encounter experience that convinces them of the truth of the Gospel. This creates openness for easier and more effective discipleship, facilitating the formation of Christlikeness in every believer.

The Importance of IHD for Effective Discipleship

The research chapter of this dissertation shows unequivocal evidence that most participants in the IHD ministry experienced an encounter with God, realignment of thoughts to the truth in God's Word, emotional healing, and restoration of their identity as sons and daughters of God loved by Him. The evidence presented by church pastors in Taiwan show that discipleship and the raising of leaders, are so much easier to achieve when IHD is incorporated. Believers who attended DEW grew in their intimacy with the Lord—many became sensitive to the Holy Spirit, experiencing and hearing Him speak to them. Like their Taiwanese counterparts, the pastors in TCC also attest to the significant changes they saw in believers, with one particularly important statement by Pastor A (mentioned earlier in the research chapter) from TCC, as follows:

> "The key advantage of DEW is in the realized benefits of a concentrated and focused time of teaching and prayer ministry. There is an intensive and focused platform for many life issues to converge and take place over several consecutive days and sessions, instead of the many aspects of life being received over the timeline of a Christian's life. During this intense focus timeframe, key thoughts are replaced and aligned with God's truth, key healing takes place, and disciples are able to think, feel, speak, act and make choices to live a life pattern that is more consistent with God's will and ways."

Considering all that has been discussed, it is time for the local churches to take ownership of the IHD ministry instead of leaving it outside of the church structure. This is a ministry of Christ that He intended for the church to continue. The IHD should be brought into the discipleship structure of the church, and not be just a "hospital unit" or "medical team" for those who ask for help. As discussed earlier, those who received help from DEW experienced being discipled with both formal teaching and prayer counseling.

IHD must become relevant for all believers. It must fulfill its role as an essential "organ" of discipleship that brings life to every believer—not just to those who are suffering. For this to happen, the design of IHD ministry (one fitting with the discipleship structure of the local church), must have some very essential elements.

These elements were actively discussed in Chapter 2. For example, there needs to be a formal teaching component that does not limit itself to merely exposing the hindrances, but which prepares the person for prayer ministry. It must have a balanced component of teaching that addresses our relationship with God, recognizing our place of submission to His Lordship and love, restoring our identity in God, revealing God's acceptance of us, and underscoring God's design for godly relationships, including God's intended order for our human sexuality. This allows for a foundation of biblical truth and instruction to continue discipleship, whether in our relationship with God, or with each other.

A second element is the existence of a prayer counseling ministry that allows for every person to safely share their lives (confidentiality and not secrecy must be provided and properly assured of). This affords an effective transformation and personal discipleship during the time of prayer counseling.

Thirdly, there needs to be a systematic follow-up after the ministry that allows a person to receive continual discipleship through accountability, mentoring, counseling, pastoral care, and psychiatric help. That a believer's progress is closely followed after receiving IHD ministry is critical. The installation of an educational bible curriculum, that empowers continued growth after attending IHD, is another important element.

Finally, a training school that helps to equip the saints to do the ministry of IHD—this itself is discipleship. As Pastor Ch from Taiwan said: "discipleship is to go and minister to others, to bring deliverance to others. Those who become DEW workers go on to minister to others. This is discipleship, specifically discipling them to minister to others." In addition, DEW builds a team of prayer counselors who are effectively empowered to wash the feet of their brothers and sisters-in-Christ.

DEW—AN IHD MODEL FOR DISCIPLESHIP

TCC is a 7,500 people strong carecell-based church with a structure of discipleship that encourages the growth of believers in being effective disciples of Christ. Every believer is encouraged to become an SP who takes responsibility in winning souls and nurturing young believers. In the process, SPs are discipled by the CLs, SLs, and ministers. The Lead Pastor takes a very active role in discipling all lay leaders through Leaders Community Empowerment (LCE) meetings. There is also an equipping and empowering arm of discipleship called Trinity Academy that creates curriculum of discipleship courses for spiritual formation, bible knowledge, and the raising of leaders. It is in this discipleship structure that DEW exists as an essential component of discipleship.

The Importance of IHD for Effective Discipleship

DEW conducts three weekends of ministry a year taking in a maximum of 120 participants each weekend. The pastors in TCC arrange for carecell members under their pastoral care to attend DEW ministry weekends. The participants are asked to read a book, Stormie Omartian's *Lord I Want To Be Whole*, before coming, as part of personal preparation. This will encourage them to trust the Lord to do something for them. During the DEW weekend, they listen to 15 hours of teaching, spanning topics such as: "Reality Check and the Love of Jesus," "The Lordship of Christ," "Authority of the Believer," "The Acceptance of God," "Rejection," "Forgiveness," "Soul-Ties" (including other religious and spiritual practices, and relationship issues), "Godly Order in Sexuality," "Generational Blessings and Curses," and "Accident and Trauma." These teachings help participants to understand the designs of God for godly living, and the nature and attending consequences of the ungodly life that they had earlier lived, which had negatively affected their relationship with God and with others, and which has robbed them of the richness of Christian living.

After these fifteen hours of teaching, personal ministry is offered to all participants by trained DEW workers. Participants always have a choice not to receive personal ministry. However, ninety-nine percent of participants opt to receive personal ministry, as the Holy Spirit shows them the concern of the Lord for their lives. Some will receive ministry during the weekend, others will come on Monday nights for ministry by the DEW ministry team.

Every participant who receives ministry is given an optional follow-up session, two to three months after the initial sessions. These sessions are important to ascertain the state of their relationship with the Lord, and the extent to which their personal lives have improved. Further ministry can be rendered during these sessions, if necessary.

Referrals for other helps may be recommended by DEW workers. These can include pastoral care, accountability, mentoring, life equipping and bible courses, books, counseling help, and psychiatric help, where necessary. The DEW pastor will relay these recommendations to other pastors to follow up with. Participants are asked to write their testimonies and a thank you letter to the Lord to affirm their healing and restoration.

Trinity Academy, works closely with DEW to arrange courses that will benefit the participants after they have received ministry. One such course usually planned for the end of the year is "The Believer's Identity in God." This is intended to reinforce and remind DEW participants of their precious identity as sons and daughters of God and to help them grow in their relationship with God. Participants are also encouraged to attend another DEW weekend teaching within a year, for a further integration of their understanding and appropriating of their new lives in God. There are other courses that Trinity Academy organizes that are relevant for their personal growth; these build upon the DEW sessions.

TOWARDS ONE GOAL ONLY

Paul says in Ephesians 4:17–24:

> So this I say, and affirm together with the Lord, that you walk no longer just as the Gentiles also walk, in the futility of their mind, being darkened in their understanding, excluded from the life of God because of the ignorance that is in them, because of the hardness of their heart; and they, having become callous, have given themselves over to sensuality for the practice of every kind of impurity with greediness. But you did not learn Christ in this way, if indeed you have heard Him and have been taught in Him, just as truth is in Jesus, that in reference to your former manner of life, you lay aside the old self, which is being corrupted in accordance with the lusts of deceit, and that you be renewed in the spirit of your mind, and put on the new self, which in the likeness of God has been created in righteousness and holiness of the truth.

IHD's role in discipleship is to partner with the Holy Spirit in His work of helping the believer set aside his old self in all of its thinking and manner of living. The believer then learns to put on the new self, "renewed in the spirit of his mind," to become the likeness of God in His righteousness and holiness of the truth. It is time for the church to take under its wing the ministry of IHD, as an integral part of its discipleship structure as intended by Jesus Christ our Lord, so that God's people may live lives that glorify the Father who loves us most.

Appendix A

Sample of Coding Exercise

CODING GROUP INTERVIEWS TAIWANESE PASTORS: SEVEN TAIWANESE CHURCHES

The seven Taiwanese churches are from Taipei, Shimen, Kaoshiung, Banqiao, Xindian, and Zhunan. These churches are a from a denominational mix that includes: Bread of Life churches, Baptist, and Presbyterian.

Question: How is DEW a part of the discipleship process?

Axial Code	Properties (Open Code/ Support Code)	Examples of participant's words
Teaching and Ministry together—effective discipleship	Blockages to growth and a way of removing them	"After DEW, I could identify root issues of my problem and had a way for removing it."
	Helps them take ownership of their life	Release the believer of wrong belief system . . . assimilate and align their thinking with biblical truths—effective renewal of the mind.

Appendix A

Axial Code	Properties (Open Code/ Support Code)	Examples of participant's words
Effective Renewing of mind for growth	Release wrong belief system Building godly belief in thoughts for growth Removing ungodly emotionally hurtful blockages to growth Understand and apply spiritual authority and start taking ownership of their life	Release the believer of wrong belief system so that they can begin to understand and assimilate and align their thinking to biblical truth, God's purpose in their lives—effective renewal of mind. Word of God and His love was locked out by strongholds of wrong belief/false belief and ungodly emotions that held me from opening my heart to God to heal my hurts . . . after DEW, I could identify root issues of my problem and had a way of removing it.

Appendix A

Axial Code	Properties (Open Code/ Support Code)	Examples of participant's words
Discipleship struggles before DEW	Unable to serve because stuck in their personal growth Discouraged	Many co-workers are passionate about serving but feel stuck in personal growth and so cannot progress in ministry and become discouraged.
	No spiritual authority to manage personal life	Helped them take up spiritual authority to take ownership of their life.
	Cannot receive God's Word and love	Cannot assimilate or align with God's Word and therefore cannot experience God's love.
	Cannot receive God's Word to lay foundation for growth	"I use to keep reading God's Word but it could not build me up nor change me."
	Lack of trust and felt manipulated and controlled by leadership	Trust has been build because they know that we are not trying to manipulate or control them.
	Absence of the experiential interaction with Holy Spirit	Before DEW they know nothing about how the Holy Spirit work in their lives.

Appendix A

Axial Code	Properties (Open Code/ Support Code)	Examples of participant's words
Discipleship struggles before DEW (*cont.*)	Difficulty serving	They are serious Christian, passionate and want to serve but somehow cannot.
	Insecure in her relationship with God	Before DEW: she was a reserved person, loved God very much, felt that God loves her very much and wanting to do many things for the Lord but because she still felt a distance between herself and God, she dare not attempt to do anything.
	Self-dependent not God-dependent	She also held on tightly to things in her life and felt that she was bounded by many things which prevented her from getting close to God.
Discipleship improvements after DEW	Have difficulty reading the bible	Cannot read bible
	Provides a wholeness for growth	Inner healing brings wholeness in people's life so that people can move towards wellness. This allows for personal breakthrough in life.
	Released from darkness to continue in light	DEW allows people to walk out of darkness into light, from brokenness into wholeness, and life renewed. She can read the Bible now. Previously she was afraid to read the Bible.
	Exercise spiritual authority to manage personal life	Spiritual Authority lesson helped him to understand and apply it to his personal life situation.

Appendix A

Axial Code	Properties (Open Code/ Support Code)	Examples of participant's words
	Could receive God's Word Able to read the Bible	Able to understand better, to accept correction and suggestions of Bible.
	Experiencing Growth	"I am now able to experience growth."
	Able to follow leadership's vision for the church (2) Trust leadership desire to for their good (4) Has real experiential interaction with the Holy Spirit	Discipleship is much easier because they are more willing to obey and conform to church, church direction and goals of the church. Area of serving—understand and align with church vision (2) They realize that we are rebuilding them via DEW and they understand that it is to bless them. Relationship of trust needed for close discipleship is build for those willing to share their personal life. This ministry builds trust because of personal sharing Leaders learn to minister to people in need and this builds relationship for discipleship
	Secure in her relationship with God (4)	After DEW—open their heart to the working of the Holy Spirit—changed persons. They experience the Holy Spirit work in their lives. She can pray now whilst previously she could not bring herself to pray.

Appendix A

Axial Code	Properties (Open Code/ Support Code)	Examples of participant's words
Discipleship improvements after DEW (*contd.*)	Experienced intimacy with God	After DEW . . . security is now fully in God
		Understand God's love . . . I feel assured by God's love and protection
		Felt assured by God's love and power through the teaching and the ministry
		Lessons allayed her fear of encountering God because of her past sins and weaknesses
		Hope in God is now a part of her life.
		Intimacy with God improved
		After DEW, hearts were opened . . . People have never been so open in their lives to the Lord.
	Experienced healing	People experienced healing in different degrees.
	Spiritual atmosphere of the church changed	There was a shift in the spiritual atmosphere of the church.
	Released to serve with enthusiasm and positive attitude (4)	After DEW—able to let God lead them, become confident and can partner others to serve.
		After DEW life changed completely. She could serve others and lead worship.
		Serving in church with a more positive attitude that was absent before DEW.

Appendix A

Axial Code	Properties (Open Code/ Support Code)	Examples of participant's words
	Released to interact with others and to love	DEW releases a person to join the community, so that the person can share in the load of the Great Commission
		A healed person can interact with others well and love others.
		Free people from shame—critical to releasing people to the Great Commission
	Sensitive to sin	Sensitive to sin
	Spiritual renewal Hope in God Released from shame and guilt	Spiritual renewal after rendering forgiveness, confession, and repentance of sin. Encountered the Lord's light shining on her and His presence. She testified that her life has gone through a major renewal.
	Marriage restoration	She was not on good terms with her husband but now marriage relationship resolved. Broke up adulterous relationship and experienced healing.
	Physical healing	Lump and pain in chest disappeared—verified by doctor.

Appendix B

Sample of Memo Constructed from Coding in Appendix A

MEMO OF TAIWANESE PASTORS GROUP INTERVIEW & WRITTEN SURVEY

Question: How is DEW a part of the discipleship process?

Appendix B

Memo #17: DEW removes the chokes that blocks discipleship process

Discipleship process often reaches a stage of stuckness in spiritual growth. Disciplers are unable to help the believer make any more progress in assimilating truth into their lives to live out their Christianity in pursuit of God's purposes in their lives. Generally, they get stuck at meeting their own needs for well-being and unable to participate in God's plan to involve them in establishing His Kingdom for the good of all mankind.

This stuckness that they experience are expressed as being insecure about their relationship with God (not sure of what God thinks about them since they think themselves not good enough for God); self-dependent and not God-dependent; self-centered living and not Kingdom-centered living; unable to take up their spiritual authority to live life; too many unresolved issues of personal hurts, failures and bondages that discourages them from venturing on in the plans of God for them (they feel that they have too much burden to deal with and have no capacity to be of any help others and serve the plans of God); lacking real interaction with the Holy Spirit and ability to believe God resulting in inability to receive God's Word; loose interest in reading God's Word; distrust leadership interest in their well-being and growth and sees leadership as simply encouraging them to fulfil leadership plans for the church.

The after-DEW effects on the believers removed many of the stuckness experienced by the believers and releases them to a renewed love and appreciation of God's work in their lives. It also gives them the freedom to serve God and to pursue His plans in establishing the Kingdom of God out of the gratitude of their hearts for His love for them.

Many who were emotionally wounded by rejections and abuse were healed by the Lord and they were able to release their past that had been an emotional burden on them. They have encountered the Lord's love in a very personal and experiential way that has awakened many of them to an experiential reality of the Holy Spirit's presence and work. Many feel assured of and secure in the love of God for them and freed from the shame and guilt of past sins. They have become enthusiastic about taking personal responsibility for their own growth, reading the Bible, and praying.

Being released from these bondages, they have stepped up to serve the Lord and many have risen up to become leaders. There is also a trust that they have now that leadership cares about them and is present to help them lay hold of God's destiny and blessings for them. This is the result of both the presence of formal teaching and the ministry that is provided in DEW. Hence, it has torn down old ungodly foundations, rebuild new foundations, and made continued discipleship after DEW easier.

Other memos made from coding of data (not referenced in Appendix A) from Taiwanese Pastors and leaders

Appendix B

Question: No formal teaching, only ministry—is DEW a part of discipleship?

> *Memo #18: Formal teaching accompanying IHD ministry makes for better discipleship.*
>
> Formal teaching makes for better discipleship because it readies the believer to receive ministry and lays foundation for growth after the ministry. The teaching helps the person understand the issues that he/she is struggling with and the possible causes of their struggles that they can bring to the Lord for healing. It also makes the believer aware that they must take ownership to how they must choose to live their lives after the ministry.
>
> Because the teaching addresses their relationship with God and the relationship issues of life, it helps them to understand how to grow right relationships with God and others. As a result of this renewed understanding, many can put aside their self-centeredness, pride, self-righteousness and improve their overall interaction with others with love.

Appendix B

Question: Any cases with negative effect or cases of backsliding after DEW? Why?

Memo #19: There are very few cases of negative effect or backsliding after DEW
There are only 1–2 known cases out of every 10-20 cases of ministry. Most of these cases have been attributed to four reasons. Firstly, the believer's ministry was incomplete because the believer was not ready to share the issues of their lives with the prayer counsellor even after hearing the teaching. Sometimes, a mismatch of prayer counsellor to participants can also be the cause of the believer not being honest about their struggles. This mismatch can be due to competency level of the DEW worker, the attitude of the counselee that makes it difficult for the DEW worker to reach out to. Secondly, the believer returns to a hostile environment that they came from without coping strategies to survive in that hostile environment resulting in them being hurt again in that environment resulting in backsliding. Thirdly, the participants did not take personal ownership to grow and take spiritual authority over their struggles and situations. Fourthly, the believer refuse special help that they need for a proper recovery such as counselling, accountability, and pastoral care, or was unavailable for follow-up assistance.

Appendix C

Sample Group Category A (Group 1 and 2), Questions on Written Interview to Leaders and Pastors

RESEARCH STUDY INTERVIEW QUESTIONNAIRE FOR PASTORS AND SECTION LEADERS

Church name:
Church address:
Pastor/Section Leader's name:
Date:

The Objective of this interview: To determine the benefits you have seen in the lives of your members and leaders whom you have send to attend the DEW Ministry and how you see DEW as part of your discipleship process.

Please be as detailed as possible in answering this interview questionnaire. However, you may leave any question that you are uncomfortable with unanswered. You may also choose to withdraw from this interview at any time with no need for any explanation.

After you have answered the questionnaire, please put it in a sealed envelope and return it to me.

As mentioned in my letter to you, only my research assistants (only apply to churches in Taiwan for Mandarin translation into English only) and myself will be reading the interviews.

I may request an oral interview with you at a later date, to clarify your reflections if necessary. You may choose not to agree to have an oral interview if you are not comfortable with it.

Appendix C

PRELIMINARY QUESTIONS

1. How long has your church been established for?
2. How many years have you been pastoring your church?
3. Describe how you have been doing discipleship in your church. Do you have a structure for raising up leaders? How do you disciple your members/leaders in the knowledge of the Word/their relationship with God/spiritual disciplines (e.g., prayer, fasting, reading the Word, service/personal life)?

INTERVIEW PROPER

Please be as detailed as possible in answering the interview questionnaire

1. When did you first send your members and leaders to the DEW ministry and what did you hope to see as a result of them attending the DEW ministry? What difficulties did you have with discipling your members/leaders before you started sending them to DEW Ministry?

2. What observable characteristics of growth/transformation have you seen in the lives of your members/leaders after they have attended the DEW ministry? What evidence of sustainable growth have you seen in the lives of your leaders after attending DEW ministry? Please share your observation of how discipleship became easier and more effective for some of your members/leaders who have attended the DEW ministry. You can name them as "Participant 1," "Participant 2," etc. Please choose a totally different person from these you have mentioned in Part B to ensure anonymity of the participant.

3. In your personal experience and understanding of the processes of the DEW ministry, what aspects (i.e., teaching/ministry session/types of prayer/removing ungodly belief system and building in godly belief system/encountering God/healing from hurts and release of pain and ungodly emotions/deliverance from demonic strongholds) of the DEW ministry process helps in the discipleship process of an individual? How does it help the discipleship process?

4. As a leader what made you convinced that inner healing and deliverance ministry is an important part of discipleship?

Appendix C

5. If the participants were only prayed for and not given the teaching portion of the ministry before receiving prayer ministry, would you still see DEW as an important part of the discipleship process of the church? Explain the reasons for your choice of "Yes" or "No."
6. What post DEW follow-up processes for the participants should DEW look at to strengthen its function as a part of the discipleship process for a local church?

Thank you for participating in my study research.

I would appreciate it if you could indicate below whether you are giving me approval to use your name and church name when referring to your written interview in writing my thesis research and paper. I will use only pseudonyms for you and your church, as mentioned in my invitation/consent letter unless you give approval to use your name and church name.

( ) Yes, you have my permission to use my name and my church's name.

( ) No, you cannot use my name or my church's name. Please use pseudonyms for my church and I.

Signature of Pastor/Section Leader:
Name:
Date:

Appendix D

*Sample Group Category B (Group 3)—
Written Interview Questionaire*

INDIVIDUAL DEW CANDIDATE WRITTEN INTERVIEW FOR PARTICIPANTS OF DEW

Name:
Church's name:
Pastor's name:
Date:

Thank you for taking the time to help me in my research study. Please fill up this written survey, after which your pastor will be conducting an interview with you. I would appreciate it if you will allow me also to have your written testimony of what the Lord has done for you.

The objective of this research interview is to determine what and how you have benefited from attending the DEW ministry, and to explore how DEW is a part of the discipleship process in a local church.

Please give as much details as possible to the questions of this interview.

QUESTIONS

1. How has the DEW teaching program and the ministry session helped you to grow as a Christian?
2. What aspects of the DEW ministry session (i.e., teaching/ministry session/removing ungodly belief system and building in godly belief systems/encountering God/healing from hurts and release of ungodly

Appendix D

and painful emotions/deliverance from demonic strongholds) helped you to grow as a Christian and how did it/they help you?

3. What did you experience during the ministry session? In what ways did you experience freedom in your mind, your emotions, your will (ability to make choices) to pursue a deeper relationship with God, and with others?

4. What obstacles to your Christian growth were removed as a result of attending DEW, that gave you the liberty to grow as a Christian and how has that removal continued to support your growth?

5. What benefits did you receive from attending DEW? What transformation, healing, change of perspectives, release, strengthening of your relationship with God and empowerment to your faith and hope in God have you experienced?

6. How has life been different for you after the DEW ministry? What changes have you experienced in your desire to grow into your maturity in Christ Jesus, and why?

7. How would you consider DEW as part of discipleship? Thank you once again for your kind assistance in my research study thesis. I would appreciate it if you will permit me to use your name and story in my research study. If you do not wish your name to be mentioned, please allow me to use your story with a pseudonym. Kindly indicate below how you would allow me to use the information that you have provided:

( ) I agree to allow the use of my name and story in your research paper.

( ) I agree to allow the use of my story but not my name. A pseudonym may be used.

Kindly sign this written survey to indicate your permission for me to use the material.

Signature:
Name:

Appendix E

Sample Identifying Benefits from Testimony and Accounts of Each Benefit

TESTIMONY OF DEW PARTICIPANT JOY*

"I have stopped struggling with a perfectionistic tendency that has hindered me from enjoying the fullest that God has for me in my life. God shows me that I need to stop striving and find full acceptance in Him. He dealt with the root causes of the tendencies to be perfect and controlling which stemmed from my early childhood experiences. He reminded me that He has always been there for me and will always be with me and that I should rely on Him and rest in Him for all the situations in my life."

TYPES OF BENEFITS IDENTIFIED AND TOTAL COUNT OF EACH BENEFIT

	Benefit	Evidence from testimony	Count
1	Being freed of negative thoughts	God shows me that I need to stop striving	1
2	Emotional healing and forgiveness	He dealt with the root causes	1
3	Release from events of past hurts	. . . from my early childhood experiences	1
4	Release from guilt/shame/failures		0

Type 1 Benefit: Removal of Hindrances

Appendix E

	Benefit	Evidence from testimony	Count
5	Personal life improvement	I have stopped struggling with . . .	1
6	Relationship Improvement		0
7	The will to live		0
8	Healthy perspective of life		1
9	Experienced peace	. . . I should rely on Him and rest in Him	1
10	Regain hope		0

Type 2 Benefit: Positive Growth in Personal Life and Relationship

	Benefit	Evidence from testimony	Count
11	Experienced encountering God's presence	God shows me . . . He reminded me . . .	1
12	Renewed faith in Christ	He has always been there for me	1
13	Growth in their intimacy with God	. . . I should rely on Him and rest in Him for all the situations in my life	1
14	Strengthening their identity in Christ		0

Type 3 Benefit: Encountering God and Renewed Faith

	Benefit	Evidence from testimony	
15	Renewed willingness to serve		0
16	Commitment to pursue God's plan and purposes for their lives		0

Type 4 Benefit: Increased Motivation to Serve God's Plans and Purposes

TESTIMONY OF DEW PARTICIPANT BOB*

"Praise God that He has shown me how He loves me for who I am—fearfully and wonderfully made by Him! I am perfect for His glory. He restored how I feel towards my mother and I forgave her. God removed the insecurity and self-condemnation in me for the relationship that I had with my girlfriend. God forgave my disobedience. God has shown me that God is my only God and I will have no other gods before Him."

Appendix E

TYPES OF BENEFITS IDENTIFIED AND TOTAL COUNT OF EACH BENEFIT

	Benefits	Evidence from the testimony	Count
1	Being freed of negative thoughts	He has shown me how He loves me for who I am . . . I am perfect for His glory	1
2	Emotional healing and forgiveness	He restored how I feel towards my mother and I forgave her	1
3	Release from events of past hurts	God removed my insecurity . . . for the relationship that I had with my girlfriend	1
4	Release from guilt/shame/failures	God removed my self-condemnation . . . forgave my disobedience	1

Type 1 Benefit: Removal of Hindrances

	Benefits	Evidence from the testimony	Count
5	Personal life improvement	He restored how I feel towards my mother	1
6	Relationship Improvement	He restored how I feel towards my mother	1
7	The will to live		0
8	Healthy perspective of life	Who I am—fearfully and wonderfully made	1
9	Experienced peace		0
10	Regain hope		0

Type 2 Benefit: Positive Growth in Personal Life and Relationship

	Benefits	Evidence from the testimony	Count
11	Experienced encountering God's presence	He has shown me how He loves me . . .	1
12	Renewed faith in Christ	He has shown me that God is my only God	1
13	Growth in their intimacy with God	I will have no other gods before Him	1
14	Strengthening their identity in Christ	God is my only God	1

Type 3 Benefit: Encountering God and Renewed Faith

Appendix E

	Benefits	Evidences from testimony	Count
15	Renewed willingness to serve		0
16	Commitment to pursue God's plan and purposes for their lives		0

Type 4 Benefit: Increased Motivation to Serve God's Plans and Purposes

* Pseudonyms used to protect anonymity.

Appendix F

Sample Second Count of Benefits According to Types

TOTALING THE COUNTS OF JOY* AND BOB*

	Benefits	Joy	Bob	Total Count
1	Being freed of negative thoughts	1	1	2
2	Emotional healing and forgiveness	1	1	2
3	Release from events of past hurts	1	1	2
4	Release from guilt, shame, failures	0	1	1
	Total Count of Type 1 Benefit: Removal of Hindrances	1	1	2

Type 1 Benefit: Removal of Hindrances

	Benefits	Joy	Bob	Total Count
5	Personal life improvement	1	1	2
6	Relationship Improvement	0	1	1
7	The will to live	0	0	0
8	Healthy perspective of life	1	1	2
9	Experienced peace	1	0	1
10	Regain hope	0	0	0
	Total Count of Type Two Benefit: Positive growth in personal life and relationship	1	1	2

Type 2 Benefit: Positive Growth in Personal Life and Relationship

Appendix F

	Benefits	Joy	Bob	Total Count
11	Experienced encountering God's presence	1	1	2
12	Renewed faith in Christ	1	1	2
13	Growth in their intimacy with God	1	1	2
14	Strengthening their identity in Christ	0	1	1
	Total Count of Type Three Benefit: Positive growth in personal life and relationship	1	1	2

Type 3 Benefit: Encountering God and Renewed Faith

	Benefits	Joy	Bob	Total Count
15	Renewal of willingness to serve	0	0	0
16	Commitment to pursue God's plan and purposes for their lives	0	0	0
	Total Count of Type 4 Benefits: Increasing motivation to serve God's plans and purposes	0	0	0

Type 4 Benefit: Increased Motivation to Serve God's Plans and Purposes

* Pseudonyms used to protect anonymity.

Appendix G

Longtitudinal Tracking of DEW Participants From a Taiwanese Church

Counselee/DEW Issues	#1	#2	#3	#4	#5	#6
1—Rejection and hurts from original family	Mother attempted to abort #1	Given away for adoption at birth	None	None	Given away for adoption	Parents divorce and abused by father
2—Bitterness and unforgiveness	Yes	Yes	Yes	Yes	Yes	Yes
3—Chinese religious idol worship (before salvation)	Yes	Yes	Yes	Yes	Yes	Yes
4—Medium and Spiritism	n/a	Yes	Yes	Yes	n/a	n/a
5—Ungodly and negative belief system	Yes	Yes	Yes	Yes	Yes	Yes
6—Generational sins	Yes	Yes	Yes	Very bad	Yes	Yes
7—Marital problems	Bad	Ok	Ok	Bad	Single	Very bad
8 -Suicidal	Yes	n/a	Yes	Yes	n/a	Yes
Role in church before DEW	Carecell leader	Believer	Believer	Believer	Believer	Believer

Appendix G

Number of DEW sessions	5	3	6	5	4	8
# of years since DEW ministry	6 years	5 years	5 years	5 years	4 years	1.5 years
Present role(s) in church	Section Leader overseeing three carecells Director of church worship team	Section Leader overseeing seven carecells Church Worship Leader	Carecell Group Leader Director of Admin Church Staff/ Associate Worship Leader	Section Leader overseeing two carecells	Carecell Group Leader Associate Worship Leader	Spiritual Parent
Key to life breakthrough	DEW and Marriage Camp	DEW	DEW	DEW	DEW	DEW and Marriage Counseling

Bibliography

Assemblies of God. "Assemblies of God 16 Fundamental Truths." https://ag.org/Beliefs/Statement-of-Fundamental-Truths.
Andrews, Alan, ed. *The Kingdom of Life*. Colorado Springs: Nav, 2010.
Andrews, Sherry. "What's Out of Sight Is Not Out of Mind." *Charisma* 2.2 (1976) 13.
Alexander, Kimberley E. *Pentecostal Healing: Models in Theology and Practice*. Dorset: Deo, 2006.
Anderson, Neil T., and Robert L. Saucy. *The Common Made Holy*. Eugene: Harvest, 1997.
Anderson, Ray S. *The Shape of Practical Theology: Empowering Ministry with Theological Praxis*. Downers Grove: InterVarsity, 2001.
Augustine. "*City of God*: Book 22.8." http://www.fordham.edu/halsall/source/augustine-cityofgod-22-9-10.asp.
Barclay, William. *The Gospel of Matthew Volume 1*. Rev. ed. Philadelphia: Westminister, 1975.
Bevans, Stephen B. "Transforming Discipleship: Missiological Reflections." *International Review of Mission* 105.402 (July 2016) 75–85.
Brown, Candy Gunter, ed. *Global Pentecostal and Charismatic Healings*, New York: Oxford University Press, 2011.
Brueggemann, Walter. "Evangelism and Discipleship: The God Who Calls, the God Who Sends." *Word & World* 24.2 (Spr 2004) 121–35.
Carroll, John T. "Sickness & Healing in the New Testament Gospels." *Interpretation* 49.2 (April 1995) 130–42.
Charmaz, Kathy. *Constructing Grounded Theory: A Practical Guide Through Qualitative Analysis*. London: SAGE, 2006.
Chaturvedi, Kanupriya. "Sampling Methods." University of Pittsburgh. http://www.pitt.edu/~super7/43011-4401/43911.ppt.
Clark, Randy. *The Biblical Guidebook to Deliverance*. Lake Mary: Charisma, 2015.
Cleansing Stream. "About Us." http://www.cleansingstream.org/about us/.
Collins, James M. *Exorcism and Deliverance Ministry in the Twentieth Century*. Eugene: Wipf & Stock, 2009.
Creswell, John W. *Qualitative Inquiry & Research Design*. London: SAGE, 2007.
———. *Research Design: Qualitative, And Mixed Methods Approaches*. 3rd ed. London: SAGE, 2009.
Daunton-Fear, Andrew. *Healing in the Early Church: The Church's Ministry of Healing and Exorcism from the First to the Fifth Century*. Eugene: Wipf & Stock, 2009.`

Bibliography

Davis, Oliver. "Transformation Theology and Pentecostalism." *Journal of Pentecostal Theology* 24.2 (Oct 2015) 172–86.
Dickinson, Robert. *God Does Heal Today*. Carlisle: Paternoster, 1995.
Duffield, Guy P., and Nathaniel M. Van Cleave. *Foundations of Pentecostal Theology*. Los Angeles: L.I.F.E. Bible College, 1983.
Elijah House, "Elijah House Training and Equipping." http://www.elijahhouse.org/page/equipping-overview.
Elwell, Walter A., ed. *Evangelical Dictionary of Theology*. Grand Rapids: Baker, 1986.
Erickson, Millard, J. *Christian Theology*. Grand Rapids: Baker, 1985.
Gaebelein, Frank E. *Romans through Galatians* Vol. 10 of *The Expositor's Bible Commentary*. Grand Rapids: Zondervan, 1976.
Glasser, Barney G., and Anselm L. Strauss. *The Discovery of Grounded Theory: Strategies for Qualitative Research*. New York: Aldine, 1967.
Glover, Dan, and Claudia Lavy. "Discipleship in the Real World." *Clergy Journal* 83.8 (August 2007) 11–13.
Hardesty, Nancy A. *Faith Cure*. Peabody: Hendrickson, 2003.
Hayward, Chris. *God's Cleansing Stream*. Ventura: Regal, 2005.
Hazard, David. "An Inside Look at Inner Healing." *Charisma* 12 (September 1986) 44–46.
Hill, Wesley. "Rethinking Christian Identity: Doctrine and Discipleship." *International Journal of Systematic Theology* 18.1 (January 2016) 120–23.
Hoekema, Anthony A. *Saved by Grace*. Grand Rapids: Eerdmans, 1994.
Horne, Charles M. *Salvation*. Chicago: Moody Bible Institute, 1971.
Horrobin, Peter. *Healing through Deliverance: Volume 1, The Foundation of Deliverance Ministry*. Grand Rapids: Chosen, 2003.
Horton, Stanley, ed. *Systematic Theology: A Pentecostal Perspective*. Springfield: Gospel, 1994.
Houston, James M. "The Future of Spiritual Formation." *Journal of Spiritual Formation & Soul Care* (Fall 2011) 131–39.
Jenny, Timothy P. "The Holy Spirit and Sanctification." In *Systematic Theology: A Pentecostal Perspective*, edited by Stanley Horton, 397–421. Springfield: Gospel, 1994.
Johnson, Susanne. "Christian Spiritual Formation in an Age of 'Whatever.'" *Review and Expositor* 98 (Summer 2001) 309–31.
Kay, William K., and Robin Parry, eds. *Exorcism & Deliverance*. Bletchley: Paternoster, 2011.
Keener, Craig. *Miracles: The Credibility of the New Testament Accounts Vol. 1*. Grand Rapids: Baker Academic, 2011.
Kelsey, Morton. *Encounter with God*. Minneapolis: Bethany Fellowship, 1988.
———. *Healing and Christianity*. Minneapolis: Augsbury Fortress, 1995.
Kim, Sean C. "*Reenchanted: Divine Healing in Korea Protestantism*." In *Global Pentecostal and Charismatic Healing*, 268–69, New York: Oxford University Press, 2011.
Kraft, Charles H. *Deep Wounds Deep Healing*. Ann Arbor: Vine, 1993.
Kydd, Ronald A. N. *Healing Through the Centuries–Models for Understanding*. Peabody: Hendrickson, 1998.
Kylstra, Betsy, and Chester Kylstra. *An Integrated Approach to Biblical Healing Ministry*. Kent: Sovereign World, Ltd., 2003.
Lang, James A. "An Evaluation of a Discipleship Process Addressing Christians' Inner Life Issues." *Christian Education Journal* 3rd Ser 12.2 (Fall 2015) 259–81.
Loranzo, N. *Unbound*. Grand Rapids: Chosen, 2003.

MacMullen, Ramsey. *Christianizing the Roman Empire (AD 100–400)*. New Haven: Yale University, 1984.
MacNutt, Francis. *Healing*. London: Hodder and Stoughton, 2001.
———. *The Healing Reawakening*. Grand Rapids: Chosen, 2005.
Maddocks, Morris. *The Christian Healing Ministry*. London: SPCK, 1991.
Mannoia, Kevin W., and Don Thorsen, eds. *The Holiness Manifesto*. Grand Rapids: Eerdmans, 2008.
Menzies, W. William, and Stanley M. Horton. *Bible Doctrines: A Pentecostal Perspective*. Springfield: Logion, 1994.
Meyer, Matthew M. "Practical Dimensions of Spiritual Growth." *Brethren Life and Thought* 34 (Spring 1989) 101–09.
Moore, Allen J. and Mary Elizabeth. "The Transforming Church: Education for a Lifestyle of Discipleship." *Impact* 9 (Fall 1982) 51–69.
Oblau, Gotthard. "Divine Healing and the Growth of Practical Christianity in China." In *Global Pentecostal and Charismatic Healing*, 320–21, New York: Oxford University Press, 2011.
Poll, Justin B., and Timothy B. Smith. "The Spiritual Self: Towards a Conceptualization of Spiritual Identity Development." *Journal of Psychology & Theology* 31.2 (2003) 129–42.
Potterfield, Amanda. *Healing in the History of Christianity*. New York: Oxford University Press, 2005.
Prince, Derek. *They Shall Expel Demons*. Tamil Nadu, India: Rhema Media Centre, 1998.
Restoring the Foundations. "Our Building Blocks." www.restoringthefoundations.org/our-building-blocks.
Restoring the Foundations. "Seminars & Events." www.restoringthefoundations.org/seminars-events/.
Richards, J. *But Deliver Us From Evil*. London: Darton, Longman and Todd, 1980.
Root, Andrew. *Christopraxis, A Practical Theology of the Cross*. Minneapolis: Fortress, 2014.
Ruthven, Jon. "The 'Imitation of Christ' in Christian Tradition: Its Missing Charismatic Emphasis." *Journal of Pentecostal Theology* 8.16 (April 2000) 60–78.
Samra, James G. "A Biblical View of Discipleship." *Bibliotheca Sacra* 160.638 (April–June 2003) 219–34.
Sandford, John Loren, and Mark Sandford. *Deliverance and Inner Healing*. Grand Rapids: Chosen, 2008.
Savage, Jeff. "Toward 2000: Renewal Through Discipleship." *American Baptist Quarterly* 15.4 (December 1996) 280–98.
Sawvelle, Bob. *A Case For Healing Today*. North Charleston: CreateSpace Independent, 2014.
Shirley, Chris. "It Takes a Church to Make a Disciple: An Integrative Model of Discipleship for the Local Church." *Southwestern Journal of Theology* 50.2 (Spring 2008) 207–24.
Stat Pac, "Survey Sampling Methods," http://statpac.com/surveys/sampling.htm
Stapleton, Ruth Carter. "The Experience of Inner Healing." *Guideposts* (1977) 7-8.
Stephens, Michael S. *Who Healeth All Thy Diseases*. Lanham, MD: Scarecrow, 2008.
Strang, Steve. "A Gift of Healing." *Charisma* 1.2 (1975) 9.
Strauss, Anselm, and Juliet Corbin. *Basics of Qualitative Research: Grounded Theory Procedures and Techniques*. Newsbury, Park: SAGE, 1990.

Bibliography

Thiessen, Henry Clarence. *Lectures in Systematic Theology*. Grand Rapids: Eerdmans, 1979.
Wardle, Terry. *Healing Care Healing Prayer*. Orange: New Leaf, 2001.
White, Heath. *Post Modernism 101*. Grand Rapids: Brazos, 2006.
White, R. E. "*Salvation*." In EDT 968.
Wilkinson, J. *Health and Healing*. Edinburgh: Handsel, 1980.
Williams, W. Joseph. *Spirit Cure*. New York: Oxford University Press, 2013.
Witcombe, John. "The History of Christian Inner Healing." https://amazingdiscoveries.org/S-deception_Sanford_Freud_Jung.
Woolmer, John. *Healing and Deliverance*. London: Monarch, 1999.
Yong, Amos, and Jonathan A. Anderson. *Renewing Christian Theology*. Waco: Baylor University Press, 2014.

www.ingramcontent.com/pod-product-compliance
Lightning Source LLC
Chambersburg PA
CBHW071454150426
43191CB00008B/1342